T0246599

HAUNTED ORLANDO

JOSHUA GINSBERG

Haunted America

Published by Haunted America
A Division of The History Press
Charleston, SC
www.historypress.com

First published 2024

Manufactured in the United States

ISBN 9781467154550

Library of Congress Control Number: 2024937576

Notice: The information in this book is true and complete to the best of our knowledge. It is offered without guarantee on the part of the author or The History Press. The author and The History Press disclaim all liability in connection with the use of this book.

*For all those we've lost,
for those who are with us still,
and, of course, for any and all
who check both of those boxes.*

*In memory of my aunt
Barbara Cohen-Kligerman.*

CONTENTS

PREFACE

Everything was leading me to write this book. At least, that's how it seems retrospectively. It has been a long and winding road for sure, but for those of you who are unfamiliar with my journey so far, indulge me, if you would, and let me quickly bring you up to speed.

Since arriving in Florida eight years ago by way of Chicago, my wife and I (along with our Shih Tzu, Tinker Bell) have been seeking out strange and unique sites and experiences, traveling the state in search of hidden history, forgotten roadside attractions and plenty of allegedly haunted hot spots. More recently, since 2020, I've had the extraordinarily good fortune to be able to turn my passion into a second act as an author and curiosity seeker. My books on the subject of offbeat local travel brought me to the attention of the leadership of the Clearwater Jolley Trolley, who asked if I might want to write some tours for them.

The first of these was a ghost tour. I took to the task happily, having reconnected with yet another one of my deep childhood fascinations.

You see, as a kid, I loved ghost stories and horror movies. As an adult, I still enjoy them, even though I consider myself respectfully skeptical of most things paranormal. But the possibilities still intrigue me, and I find that some part of me, like Fox Mulder, wants very much to believe. Perhaps one day I…

Wait! Wait—what was that? Did you see that?

Did the lights just flicker and dim? From the very corner of your eye, did you spy a shadow ever so casually slip loose from the object to which it was anchored and slink away of its own volition? Did the unmistakable sound of footsteps on the floor approaching you suddenly stop short the very moment you became fully aware of them?

You can tell yourself, as I have many times while researching and writing the stories in this book, that surely, it's just your imagination playing tricks on you; it's only a draft making you shiver and raising the hairs on the back of your neck. You can say out loud, if it helps, that there must always be some rational explanation.

All the same, perhaps we'll leave the night light on tonight and keep some salt and a holy symbol forged of iron within arm's reach on the nightstand.

Because no matter what we believe or disbelieve, our faith goes only so far. And not even we skeptics can be truly certain of who or what might come through when we open the door to that which is unknown and unknowable.

ACKNOWLEDGEMENTS

I t occurs to me that writing a book and ghost hunting have at least one important feature in common: the success of both endeavors depends on the active participation of (usually) unseen presences. So, allow me to briefly pull back the veil and shine a light on just some of those hidden hands that played such a critical role in making the book you're now reading a reality.

First, thank you to Joe Gartrell and everyone at Arcadia/The History Press for being so receptive and supportive throughout the process, from my initial pitch to proofreading and production. I could not be happier with the product or with this new relationship.

I also want to thank Ting Rappa and her team at American Ghost Adventures for providing exceptional insight and guidance. Being able to access their knowledge and firsthand experiences was a tremendous boon. The same goes for Pamela Redditt at the Cottage Gift Shop, Greg Piecora at Wops Hops Brewing and many others, who kindly shared their personal experiences with me. Thanks are also owed to Emilio San Martin and Daniel Ortiz from the Orlando Paranormal Investigations (OPI) Facebook group, both of whom reviewed my work. Additionally, organizations such as the Orange Country Regional History Center and the Sanford Museum were helpful and enthusiastic in offering their insight and suggestions.

As the latest in a very long line of those writing about Orlando's haunted history, I want to thank all of those authors whose books I referred to frequently and have listed in the bibliography and to all of the paranormal investigators whose research I consulted.

And of course, there are all the many friends and family who were once again subjected to reading and rereading the numerous drafts of this book, especially Howard and Debbie Weiner, who went way beyond any reasonable expectations by serving as proofreaders. Thank you to Andy and Bob, David and Myrna, Ali, Jeremy, Seth and Adam for the familial love and support. Also deserving of recognition are my friends, including Candi Orchulek and Tom McElroy, Glenda Ganung, the Tiger Dust folks (Jason, Laura, Eddie, Trent and all), Michael Lortz, Craig Pittman, Gary Silber, Matt McMonigle and Bailey, Andrew Tschudy and Kiefer, Aaron Feldman, Jason Ewing, Larry Hayward, Bobby Conway and Mehul Soni. Ample gratitude goes to my various employers (who are all very understanding of my curious habits and strange schedule), including the Studio at Grant Thornton, Mary Dismore of Your Signature Resume and my Reedy Press family, with whom I began and continue my literary adventures. And thank you very much to all of my talented new friends and fellow authors within the Southwest Florida chapter of the Horror Writers Association for providing a limitless supply of wonderfully dark and twisted inspiration.

Lastly, thank you to my wife, partner and coconspirator, Jen, and our canine companion Tinker Bell the Shih Tzu for making every day the adventure I enjoy most.

INTRODUCTION

First and foremost, thank you for joining me on this latest leg of my journey, which takes us not on a tour of all the weird, wonderful and obscure locations in and around Orlando but, more specifically, into the area's haunted hot spots and ghostly legends.

Being able to shift gears a bit and find yet one more facet through which to explore and understand a place has been both a tremendous honor and a significant challenge. In fact, of the books I've written thus far, the one you're holding in your hands has been unquestionably the most difficult. At times, as I rewrote certain portions for the third, fourth or fifth time, admittedly, it felt (appropriately) as though I was wrestling with some unseen force that would neither rest nor allow me to rest until I'd gotten all the stories right.

And getting the stories right was not always easy. For one thing, it was a matter of finding the right balance between a history book focused on hauntings and a book of ghost stories that shines a light deeper into local history. My hope is that the result can be read either way. I've also tried to infuse some humor and more than a few geeky pop culture references, all while remaining respectful. Every ghost story, after all, is spawned from a human life lost, and that's worth pausing to consider. Whether you believe in the supernatural or not, nearly all of the ghosts in this book presumably left behind grieving friends, families and colleagues.

Bearing this in mind, there was also the challenge of chasing down local legends and lore. Since many of these stories had been passed on by word of mouth, sometimes for generations, getting to the underlying historical facts was often difficult and, in some cases, not possible at all. As with any orally transmitted tale, this meant that variations and conflicting accounts emerged from one retelling to another. To the extent possible, I've endeavored to capture those alternative versions, thereby allowing readers to decide for themselves what sounds most credible and what seem less so. Also, ghosts, being the most liminal sort of things, tend to go hand in hand with places that are equally liminal. Brothels, opium dens and other such places would, for the most part, have been left off the lists of legitimate businesses, even during the time in which they operated.

These difficulties were further complicated by the endlessly changing nature of Orlando and pretty much all of Central Florida for that matter. The pace at which businesses come and go and buildings are erected, remodeled and leveled is generally mind-boggling, but it seems to have further accelerated since the COVID-19 pandemic. Counties break apart, cities change their names and those old buildings lucky enough to be preserved are very often moved from where they originally stood. All of this makes finding them, let alone telling stories about them, a rather daunting undertaking. Of course, even with the best of intentions and a commitment to getting it right, ultimately, I bear full responsibility for any errors or inconsistencies. I hope you won't find any of those, but if you do, please let me know, and I will do my best to correct them in future editions.

In assembling this work, I read dozens of books on the subject, reviewed easily over one hundred articles and videos shared online and talked to countless individuals, both on and off the record. The result was that I ended up with reams of notes and vastly more stories than I could ever include in a volume even three times the size of this one. I tried to choose the stories that seemed the most historically significant, the ones that fit together to tell a story not just of ghosts but also of Orlando itself. Just as often, that meant digging into the stories I hadn't heard before, the ones that had not been, to my knowledge, previously recorded. And I tried to apply some sensitivity as well. On one hand, I didn't shy away from talking about tough subjects, like the Ocoee Massacre, in which an unknown number of Black residents were killed for trying to exercise their voting rights. On the other hand, there were some wounds that just seemed too deep and too recent to probe— specifically the Pulse Nightclub shooting. So, I looked to another author's words to help guide me in determining what to include and what to exclude.

In *Ghostlands: An American History in Haunted Places*, author Colin Dickey, at one point, discusses the distinction that Kishwahili speakers make between two different types of dead—the *sasha*, who are recently departed and whose lives overlapped with those still living, and the *zamani*, who are no longer remembered by anyone living. The victims of the Pulse shooting are and will for many years to come be in that first category. For that reason, I felt that they and the victims of some other, more recent tragedies were off limits. I encourage everyone to visit the Pulse Nightclub memorial, but as a courtesy, leave the ghost hunting equipment behind. Anyone wishing to communicate with the dead there can best do so by leaving a message or memory on the community wall.

A brief note on technical stuff. I assume that most readers are familiar with the various categories of hauntings (residual, intelligent, poltergeist, object hauntings, demonic activity, shadow people, vortexes and portals, et cetera), so I haven't spent much ink on covering what is better and more fully explained elsewhere. The same goes for all the various tools and technologies used by professional ghost hunters (ranging from dousing rods to flashlights, K2 meters, infrared cameras, video and audio recorders, spirit boxes and the like). There has been a trend toward including psychics on paranormal investigative teams, and it should be noted that I use the terms *psychic* and *sensitive* somewhat interchangeably. I also alternate between *ghost* and *spirit* when using those terms broadly.

There's just one last point I want to be sure to include here. Yes, I appreciate the vaguely subversive thrill of exploring old and abandoned places, but I always do so safely and with permission. For one thing, the idea of being trapped in an underground tunnel or crashing through the floor of a rotting building somewhere is just not something I have any interest in doing. Nor do I have any interest in (or budget for) paying hospital bills or fines associated with trespassing or breaking and entering. If there is one thing I implore of you, it is to use good judgement and be safe. Even if you're an experienced ghost hunter or tour guide, I hope and assume that you will do everything in your power to avoid becoming the very thing you seek and ending up in some future edition of this book as a cautionary tale for others.

That's it—that's all I wanted to say. So, be safe, have fun, be respectful and maybe I'll see you on the other side—of the book, that is.

1

DOWNTOWN ORLANDO

For thousands of years prior to the arrival of Europeans, Central Florida was inhabited by various Indigenous peoples. In the Orlando area, these people included the Timucua and, later on, the people known as the Seminoles, a group composed of Creek and other tribes pushed south as the United States expanded from its original colonies. The Spaniards and the English had both visited Florida (generally in the most bloodthirsty and gold-obsessed manner, which did not endear them to the locals), each claiming it for a time and both finding it to be a more or less unmanageable nightmare of a swamp complete with swarms of disease-carrying mosquitoes and giant man-eating lizards.

It was during the Seminole Wars in 1838, as Florida was transitioning from a wild territory into the twenty-seventh state in the United States (which was annexed on March 3, 1845), when the first soldiers arrived to occupy Fort Gatlin, just south of what would become Orlando.

The 1840s saw the small community there come to be known as Jernigan after the first family who formed a permanent settlement there. The name was made official when the post office was established there in 1850. Six years later, the town expanded north and took on the name it's known by today: Orlando. The prevailing story is that the town was given the name in honor of the heroic sacrifice made by a soldier named Orlando Reeves, who awakened his companions to a Seminole surprise attack at the cost of his own life. That story, however, is almost certainly apocryphal, and the true origin story of the city's name is unknown (alternate theories include

Judge James Speer having been a fan of Shakespeare or, just as likely, wanting the city named after a friend).

What everyone can agree on is that Orlando's first big industry was cattle. The railroads brought the first significant transformation to the area, and the population began to grow by leaps and bounds during the Reconstruction era after the Civil War. Orlando was officially incorporated on July 31, 1875, and was reincorporated as a city just six years later. By this time, the citrus industry had taken root in Florida, and Orlando had become one of its major hubs.

Photograph of downtown Orlando, taken in 1957 by Jim Stokes. *Courtesy of Florida Memory, State Library and Archives of Florida.*

The 1920s saw a major Florida land boom as Orlando and the rest of the state gained popularity as an idyllic place to vacation. This growth was not destined to last, though. It ended with disasters, both natural (hurricanes) and economic (the Great Depression). Many of the vacant resorts were filled again with airmen training for combat during World War II, after which the area continued to grow. NASA made Cape Canaveral a major launch site, and shortly thereafter, the mouse came to town, once more transforming the Orlando area and leading to the city we recognize today.

Over time, Orlando has seen conflict, booms and busts and tragedies both minor and major. Blood and tears, love, loss and redemption—all of these are components not only of the city's history but also of its stories. The most memorable of those stories, the ones that get retold and passed down from generation to generation, are, some would say, the ghost stories.

BRINGING THE PAST BACK TO LIFE: ORANGE COUNTY REGIONAL HISTORY CENTER

It stands to reason that hauntings are most likely to occur where something tragic took place. Often, but not always, this is the very worst sort of tragedy, specifically the loss of human life, although a place where justice was meted out, where families and loved ones were separated and sentenced, would certainly also qualify. If that's so, then few buildings in Orlando have seen

Exterior of the Orange County Regional History Center. *Photograph by the author.*

as much tragedy play out within their walls as the former Orange County Courthouse. The current Beaux-Arts–style building designed by Murray S. King was erected in 1927 in the vicinity of previous judicial buildings. The building, having outlived its original function, has enjoyed an afterlife of its own as the Orange County Regional History Center, opened to the public in September 2000. Since that time, according to professional ghost hunters as well as staff members at the museum, regular visitors include more than just the corporeal crowds who pass through during the day.

Given the building's past function as well as its present purpose in preserving the past, it's not surprising that such a temporal nexus would spawn a multitude of alleged hauntings. Two events related to the building's days as a courthouse are worth highlighting in this regard.

The first of these, which is likely the best known, began on January 7, 1980, when notorious serial killer Ted Bundy was tried for the murder of twelve-year-old Kimberly Diane Leach in the third-floor courtroom. Leach, who vanished from her school in the middle of the day, is believed to have been the last of the thirty victims whose deaths Bundy confessed to. In spite of the insanity plea put forward by Bundy's attorneys, the jurors still found

Image of Ted Bundy in court in Florida. *Wikimedia Commons.*

the killer sane enough to receive a guilty verdict one month later. Bundy was then sentenced to death for the second time.

There have been numerous reports of an apparition in the courtroom and the hall, sounds of pacing footsteps and reports of objects seemingly moving of their own volition. Some have connected this abundance of activity to a large wooden table where Bundy's name was carved into one corner. While it makes for compelling ghost story gristle, the name was almost certainly left there by someone other than the serial killer himself. For one thing, Bundy's trial took place not in the preserved courtroom on the third floor of the building but rather in the adjoining annex, which was closed in 1989 due to asbestos and then demolished in 1998. It is unlikely that the desk was moved from the annex, as photographs reveal furniture of a more modern style than the desk in question. Yet another argument against Bundy having carved his name on anything anywhere in the building has to do with heightened security. Having previously escaped twice from prison, Bundy was under constant supervision that would have made it all but impossible for him to have brought with him any implement sharp enough to carve his name, let alone do it unobserved.

If the story of the name being carved by Bundy is apocryphal, what about the spirit (or spirits) connected to the courtroom? Do those belong to the infamous killer? Among those who believe the story to be unlikely is Ting Rappa, founder and owner of Orlando-based American Ghost Adventures who is herself sensitive to the presence of spirits. Few if any individuals have spent as much time as she seeking out and communicating with ghosts within and beyond the building. While she recognizes the impulse to try to connect hauntings to the ghosts of the famous and infamous, she believes that, more likely, the apparition and sounds of pacing inside the courtroom are connected to a juror who died of a heart attack before he could deliver his verdict. The matter, which weighed heavily on him in life, continues to deny him peaceful eternal slumber.

Rappa finds far more substance in the connection between the hauntings at the history center and a separate incident from its courthouse days involving

This page: The doorway and interior of the courtroom preserved inside the Orange County Regional History Center. *Photographs by the author.*

a convicted murderer named Thomas Harrison Provenzano. On January 10, 1984, Provenzano entered the courthouse intent on finding and confronting the officer who had charged him five months earlier with disorderly conduct. He carried with him a shotgun, an assault rifle and a revolver, as well as ammunition, and when he was approached by two bailiffs, he opened fire. Sixty-year-old Deputy Arnold "Arnie" Wilkerson was killed on the spot, and fifty-three-year-old Deputy Sheriff Harry Dalton was severely wounded and died seven years later from the injuries he sustained that day. Nineteen-year-old Correctional Officer Mark Parker was also paralyzed after using his body to shield a civilian from the gunfire; he expired in 2009 from complications related to his injuries. The deranged Provenzano was himself put to death by lethal injection on June 21, 2000.

The impact of this tragedy can still be felt in more ways than one. The most noticeable change was that, largely as a result of this incident, metal detectors were installed in government buildings throughout the country. Some, however, believe that there is another, less obvious aftereffect, which is that at least one of those who died from Provenzano's bullets remains on duty, guarding and protecting the building in the afterlife. Rappa recalls an experience she had while alone, exploring one of the hallways of the building. She heard a distinctly male voice beside her very clearly ask, "Can I help you?" Is this the voice of Arnie or one of his colleagues continuing to keep watch over the living? Rappa believes it very well might be.

The most frequently documented and encountered ghost at the museum, however, has nothing to do with any specifically known court cases or incidents that took place at the site. This would be the spirit known as Emily, a young girl believed to be between seven and eight years old who wears a white dress and keeps her dark hair tied in pigtails. She is believed to have been removed from the care of an abusive father and an unfit mother and made a ward of the state, making the old courthouse likely the last place she saw her parents. While multiple investigators and psychics have interacted with Emily, Rappa and her team have gone further and established a relationship with her.

The presence of a young girl's spirit was made known to Rappa when she began investigating the building in 2004. Initially, she explained, she was using fairly simple tools, including electromagnetic field (EMF) detectors and highly sensitive flashlights that sentient spirits are thought to be able to turn on and off in answer to questions. Over time, Rappa and her team's interactions with Emily evolved alongside the technologies they use today, which include audio recorders to capture electronic voice phenomenon (EVP), thermal imaging cameras and spirit boxes.

Communication with Emily began playfully enough with the disembodied sounds of giggling, laughter and an occasionally glimpsed, full-bodied apparition peeking over a railing, seemingly curious about those with whom she was now sharing the former courthouse and museum. Rappa and her colleagues began leaving small objects out for Emily, including candy and animal crackers, which she seemed especially fond of, according to a guide by the name of Robert.

Later on, there was an overnight slumber party at the museum as part of a summer camp for kids. They brought with them blankets and, in some cases, treasured toys and personal items. It was after this event that Rappa's team determined Emily wanted a toy of her own, so they provided her with her own miniature teddy bear.

The story related by Rappa is that during a particularly cold December night, one of her ghost tour guides inadvertently stuffed Emily's teddy bear into a bag of her personal belongings and equipment, removed it (and Emily) from the building and left it in her car. Emily was most displeased about this turn of events, so much so that she started causing trouble for that particular tour guide by disrupting various electrical devices the guide came into contact with, such as her television, hair dryer and car (the same one with the teddy bear in it). Once Emily's teddy bear was discovered and returned to the museum, all of the guide's electrical issues were resolved as quickly as they had begun.

Around the same time, Rappa added a psychic to her team. On entering the Orange County Regional History Center—and without knowledge of any of the specifics about the team's relationship with Emily—this new team member immediately identified the ghost of a young girl jumping up and down with excitement at seeing Rappa and her team. With permission from the spirit, he began channeling, making himself a conduit for more direct communication. They (Emily and the medium) turned first to the guide who had accidentally forgotten the teddy bear and said to her, "I had to teach you a lesson. It's my toy!" Next, the spirit addressed Robert and asked, "Why don't you ever bring frosted animal crackers anymore?" Apparently, at some point, he had ceased leaving treats for Emily.

Historically, the channeling of spirits by mediums and psychics hasn't always risen to what most would consider the threshold of irrefutable proof of something supernatural. In this case, at least, it certainly is compelling, especially when one considers the preponderance of so many other firsthand accounts and experiences.

IN BETWEEN PLACES: THE GHOSTS OF WALL STREET PLAZA

Just across North Court Avenue from the Orange County Regional History Center is Wall Street Plaza, which runs alongside the historic Angebilt Hotel. Once the sun sets, the plaza comes to life as part of the downtown bar and club scene, with music and guests spilling into and out of establishments like Hooch, the Hen House Bar, Waitiki and the Wall Street Cantina. But if reports are to be believed, it isn't just the restaurants and watering holes located here that are reanimated each night.

Stories of strange happenings and hauntings seem to have started circulating and filtering into the public consciousness sometime during the 1990s. In 1991, when Barrie Freeman and William Waldren came together to open the coffee shop Yab Yum (a reference to the novel *The Dharma Bums*, which author Jack Kerouac finished while living in Orlando). The coffeehouse was a hit and evolved into multiple ventures there in the plaza under the Yab Yum Inc. umbrella. These included the Kit Kat Club, the Globe Restaurant and Harold and Maude's Espresso Bar.

Of the establishments located there in the plaza, the Kit Kat Club, which closed in 2001, has tended to be the focus of ghost hunters and paranormal enthusiasts. In addition to numerous eyewitness accounts of bottles flying from their places on the shelves behind the bar, some have recounted unusual experiences they had in the women's bathroom there. Author Thomas Cook, who previously documented some of Orlando's better-known haunts, wrote that some experienced a sense of uneasiness, while one individual watched in horror as her own face in the mirror rapidly aged fifty years.

The apparition of a woman in a long black dress descending a rear staircase has been cited by multiple sources, some of which place her at Harold and Maude's; still others recall seeing her at the Kit Kat Club. Could it be that this lady in black was alternating her visits between both of these establishments? Certainly, she was dressed in the color fashionable in both the clubs and coffeehouses at the time.

Might this posthumous patron clad in black be the same individual who paid one employee of Harold and Maude's a different sort of late-night visit? According to Cook, one female employee who was alone at the coffee shop after closing heard the sound of the front door unlock followed by heavy footfalls entering the shop. After emerging from the back room to investigate, this individual found no one present and nothing amiss, so she returned to her duties. When it happened a second time, however, she decided to call it a night and depart with haste.

Wall Street Plaza during the day is rather quiet, but at night, it is packed with tourists and revelers. *Photograph by the author.*

The coffeehouse Yab Yum was also at the center of at least one paranormal incident, when a manager there discovered for herself that more was brewing there than just dark roast. The story goes that while she was working on a display at the coffeehouse one night, she had the keen sense of being watched. After a quick search, she was satisfied that she was alone and returned to work. A bit later, the manager again felt a presence behind her, just over her shoulder, while she was doing some work in front of a large mirror. She spun around and again confirmed that she was alone. When she turned to face the mirror, however, she saw the reflection of a teenage girl, presumed to be the spirit of a homeless girl who had resided in the building during one of its earlier incarnations as a theater.

Is there some underlying reason for all of the disturbing and unexplained activity at this location? Some, like Cook, suggest that the answer might be found right across the street on a historical marker erected in 2019, which tells, on one side, the story of the lynching of July Perry and, on the other side, explains, more broadly, racial violence in America.

The tragic events that led to what's known as the Ocoee Massacre began on November 3, 1920, when Mose Norman and other Black residents were turned away from voting in the heavily Ku Klux Klan–controlled area. Undeterred, after consulting with Orlando judge John Cheney, Norman made a second attempt to cast his vote. This time, he was violently assaulted by armed white men who were guarding the polling place. He fled to the home of his friend July Perry, who was wounded when a mob showed up and burned the house. Perry was sent to the Orange County Jail in Orlando, where, the next morning, he was taken by a lynch mob, beaten and hanged near Judge Cheney's home. Perry's lifeless body was further riddled with bullets. The racial violence spilled over into Ocoee, where some twenty-five Black homes, two Black churches and a Masonic lodge were razed. Estimates on the loss of life range from six to over thirty, making it one of the saddest and bloodiest days in American political history.

Julius July Perry. *Associated Press.*

No one was ever held responsible. The Black community never recovered, and within a year, the survivors had been forced to sell their land and homes. The suspected ringleader of the mob became the mayor of Ocoee, and as with the racial violence elsewhere in the state, at Rosewood, it would be nearly a generation before the Ocoee Massacre was discussed in anything more than hushed tones.

So, how does this all connect with Wall Street Plaza? That, according to historians, is where the Orange County Jail stood, the place from which Perry was taken by force to be lynched. Perry's body was laid to rest in Greenwood Cemetery. For over eighty years, his grave was unmarked until he was given a headstone in 2002. Around that same time, reports of ghostly activity in and around Wall Street Plaza declined sharply. While some consider it purely coincidental, others choose to take it as a sign that the spirits of Perry and other victims of the massacre are finally at peace, having at last been recognized and remembered.

WHAT LIES BENEATH: THE ANGEBILT BUILDING

The 1920s, also known as the New Era, the Jazz Age and the Roaring Twenties, was, for many, a time of economic growth, when middle-class and wealthy Americans saw their incomes and standards of living increase. From the mix of prosperity and prohibition came a unique and memorable cast of characters, not least of whom were flappers, mobsters and the fictional Jay Gatsby.

Joseph Fenner Ange fit none of those archetypes. He grew up on a farm in North Carolina, attended country schools and learned the carpentry trade before becoming a contract builder. The year 1913 found him newly arrived in Orlando, where he set about erecting numerous buildings. He also served as the first vice-president of the Bank of Orange and Trust Company. Later, he became the primary organizing force behind the Orlando Mortgage and Loan Company as well as the president of the Orange Hotel Company. It was in that last capacity that he bestowed upon Orlando the first-class hotel to which he affixed his own name: the Angebilt.

Located at 37 North Orange Avenue, the eleven-story building was the tallest in Orlando when it opened on March 14, 1923. To bring his vision to life, Ange hired architect Murray S. King, who modeled the building after New York City's Pennsylvania Hotel. Complete with a lobby, lounge, spa, dining room, parlor, bridal room, barbershop and rooftop deck, the 250-room hotel's prices ranged from four dollars a night for a single room with a bath to twenty dollars a night for a suite.

Exterior of the Angebilt building. *Photograph by the author.*

Just two months after opening his hotel, however, Ange sold his interest in it, and the hotel declared bankruptcy in June 1923. It was sold at public auction and reopened and went on to host a number of big celebrities, including Harvey Firestone, Henry Ford and Thomas Edison. In the 1960s, Joan Crawford held a reception there for Pepsi Co., of which she was a board member.

The hotel's difficulties stand in stark contrast to its successes over the years. In 1944, the rooftop deck was destroyed by a hurricane. Before the end of the 1960s, the hotel had gone into a downward spiral, its once glamorous occupants replaced by transients, sex workers and other unsavory guests. Despite the hotel having once been billed as "fireproof," on February 27, 1983, a fire broke out and consumed its top two floors. The hotel never recovered and was converted to an office building. In the 1990s, while the Orange County Courthouse was moving to its new location, it temporarily made use of the Angebilt, after which the building was again occupied by commercial tenants. Though the Angebilt never served as a hotel again, some who have worked in and visited the building over the years suggest that it might still be receiving guests, albeit not the flesh-and-blood kind.

The lobby of the Angebilt building. *Photograph by the author.*

So, then, what about the ghosts? An article from the Orange County Regional History Center describes a variety of activity, including individuals in bathroom stalls discovering that the doors refused to unlock and opened while the walls of the stalls shook violently. One such hapless individual described having to crawl out under the stall to escape.

As recently as September 2023, a similar experience was posted online by someone who had started work on the third floor of the building just a few months earlier. Working late one night, around 8:00 p.m., the individual stepped out of their office to use the restroom. Upon returning, they shut their office door and resumed work, but shortly thereafter, the door opened a crack. Thinking it was just a faulty lock, they shut the door, making sure it was firmly latched, only to have the door unlock and again swing open. They watched as the door moved back and forth several times despite confirming that the air-conditioning was turned off and there was no discernable draft in the hallway.

Another documented situation involved a manager who had to enter the building over the weekend to handle a work emergency. While ascending to the upper floors, she had the uncanny feeling of being watched, even though she was certain she was alone. While she worked at her desk, she began hearing strange and unexpected sounds—snippets of conversation, laughter, clinking glasses and other temporal echoes perhaps of some long-since-ended party. She assumed these to be noises from outside and continued her work, only to be interrupted shortly thereafter by a loud knocking on her door. She opened the door and peered out into a silent, empty hallway. She explored the hallway further, unable to locate any other unlocked doors or nooks in which someone could be hiding. Having confirmed to her satisfaction that she was, indeed, alone on the floor, she started back toward her office. The sound of giggles and high-pitched laughter coming from the vacant hallway stopped her in her tracks. While it is unclear if she got any more work done that day, it is certain that from that day forth, she never worked alone in the building again.

These experiences on the building's upper floors may represent just the tip of the bone-chilling iceberg. The overwhelming majority of paranormal activity associated with the building centers on a secret underground tunnel that connects the old hotel to the Beecham Theater across Orange Avenue (which, incidentally, is said to have its own ghost of the "lady in white" variety). A trapdoor behind the stage of the theater was allegedly used to transport top-tier, A-list talent unseen between the hotel and the venue. The tunnels are a tight squeeze in places, however, which leads some historians to posit that the passageway was put to another use—as a place to hide liquor during Prohibition. At least one source has suggested that the tunnel was used to transport dangerous criminals while the building was being used by the Orange County Courthouse, but the only evidence to support this claim has thus far been anecdotal.

There may be little agreement on how and by whom the secret subterranean passageway was used in the past, but many paranormal investigators and ghost hunters share the opinion that there is indeed something residing there now amid the clutter and debris.

Some who have entered the tunnels report having been overcome with a sense of dread so strong that they need to retreat. Others brave enough to hold EVP sessions at the entranceway to the tunnels claim to have generated interesting results. According to Whitehead, one individual vowed never to set foot near the tunnels again after being chased out by "a low, guttural voice." Whitehead and others believe that the activity here is more indicative of demonic (nonhuman) rather than ghostly activity.

RISING FROM THE ASHES: THE GHOST OF EDWARD KUHL

Most cities have certain key moments in their development to which history returns time and again. For Orlando, one of these is the Great Fire of the late nineteenth century that devastated its small business district. That fire began in the predawn hours of January 12, 1884, inside the grocery store owned by James Delaney at the corner of Pine Street and Magnolia Avenue. Although no lives were lost, the fire spread through the small business district and, in its aftermath, reshaped downtown Orlando. Those changes included the establishment of a fire department as well as new building codes, and for local businessman Edward Kuhl, it meant rebuilding. At 69 East Pine Street, where the devastating blaze began, Kuhl and Delaney erected the Kuhl-Delaney building, also known as the Phoenix building (which was appropriate, as it had literally risen from the ashes at that address). Kuhl, a German immigrant who arrived in Orlando in 1873 by way of Mississippi after serving in the Confederate army, went on to operate a candy store, serve as the first president of the Orlando Board of Trade, donate land for the county road into Kissimmee (which was named Kuhl Avenue at the time) and built a second, three-story building across from the Phoenix.

Kuhl's success was memorable but ultimately short-lived. Just four years after the fire, on May 25, 1888, the businessman suffered a fatal heart attack while going up the stairs to his third-floor office across from the Phoenix building. Kuhl, who was just forty-five years old at the time of his death, no doubt left behind a great deal of unfinished business, which could account for the abundance of ghostly activity at the building. One could say that, even in death, Kuhl continues to be something of an overachiever.

Evidence that Kuhl is still hands-on with the various ventures that have come and gone under the roof of his old building includes reports of glasses sliding off bar counters; bottles disappearing, only to reappear moments later; and boxes being stacked in improbable ways that differ from how they had been left the night before. These happenings were frequent enough that the former Ghost Bar and Lounge decided to make Kuhl's ghost an integral part of its marketing. In an online article, the establishment claimed it was "home to ghost Edward Kuhl, original owner/builder" and that the name of the business was "a nod to resident ghost Edward Kuhl, who's more mischief than malice."

Another individual who believes that Kuhl is responsible for poltergeist-style shenanigans is Ting Rappa, who related a few different incidents in the book *In the Shadow of Two Theme Park Castles* that she and Debra Walloch Hoffman collaborated on. One of these involved a light fixture over a bar, from which the bulb would constantly vanish, only to be rediscovered in unexpected places, such as employees' handbags and ice buckets. The manager decided to mark the bulb with an "x" in order to track its unexplained travels, which included it somehow showing up inside a sealed and unopened box of supplies.

There's also the story of the preschool-aged son of one of the previous lounge owners. The boy's parents were slightly puzzled when the boy, who regularly accompanied them to work, made what they believed was an imaginary friend in the building. The boy insisted, however, that his friend was real (incorporeal, it should be noted, is not the same as imaginary) and described him as a kindly older gentlemen named Eddie.

Rappa believes that Eddie (who she says prefers that name or Edward but never Mr. Kuhl) also pranked two of her own American Ghost Tour guides who were leading a tour through the building one night in 2016. Eddie had been communicative that evening, interacting with the group by turning on and off various flashlights, and after some time there, the guides gathered all of the equipment, including exactly ten K2 meters, before moving on to the next location. When they arrived at the next destination though, they discovered that one of the meters (valued at roughly sixty dollars) had gone missing. After emptying the gear bag and checking all possible pockets and pouches, the meter could not be found. So, the two guides decided to return to the Kuhl building, where they made a full sweep (including in the area around the lightbulb that Eddie liked to hide). Still, they found nothing left in the building, but when they checked their gear bag one final time, the tenth meter had mysteriously returned.

If Eddie is indeed still present at his former address, it seems that death has done nothing to diminish his playful and puckish (if slightly kleptomaniacal) nature. Those who chose to explore the matter further might want to keep a close watch on their personal items.

MISTER ROGERS'S HAUNTED HOOD: THE ROGERS BUILDING

Pause for a moment and ask yourself: Are some buildings prone—even destined—to become haunted? When a structure is first planned and erected, no one can predict what human experiences and memories will come to fill it, what joys and tragedies will play out within its walls, what memories will be forged under its ceilings and which of those might remain long after the inhabitants have moved on. Aside from all of the individual and family histories that can amount to a haunting (in either fact or folklore), are there specific things about a place that makes it "ghost friendly"? Age is a factor, of course. It stands to reason that the older the building, the greater the number of people who've passed over its threshold, each perhaps leaving some part of themselves and adding to the layer of metaphysical fingerprints. Another commonality between many allegedly haunted buildings, according to author Colin Dickey, is that they are somehow architecturally unique, distinct or otherwise unusual or memorable.

Regarding longevity and uniqueness, the Rogers building, located at 37 South Magnolia Avenue, checks both of those boxes.

Built in 1886, it is considered the area's oldest building, erected just two years after the Great Orlando Fire of 1884 ravaged the downtown area, destroying several buildings, including the one that housed the *Orange County Reporter*. The city rebuilt, establishing a fire department and enforcing the rule that future structures be constructed of "fireproof" materials, such as brick and concrete, rather than wood. Interestingly, the Rogers building still managed to retain a wooden frame, the last (and, today, the only) such building in the city.

Exterior of the Rogers building.
Photograph by the author.

Along with its longevity, the building is architecturally unique for a number of reasons. The Queen Anne–style building, created by architect William H. Mullins, features forest green–painted zinc siding (a curious choice given Florida's heat and humidity) that was allegedly shipped from England. In 1983, it was added to the National Register of Historic Places, and today, it is also an Orlando Historic Landmark.

The building takes its name from Gordon Rogers, the English settler for whom it was designed. It served as his grocery and liquor store, and it also became a gathering place for fellow British expatriates. That second function for the space was made official with the establishment of the English Club, located on the building's second floor. Given the times, it was, predictably, a gathering place exclusively for men.

Since that time, the building has seen use in at least a dozen other ways as a restaurant, a coffeehouse, a beauty shop, an Arthur Murray Dance Studio, an art gallery and the theater and home base for the Mad Cow Theater Company. In 2018, Ford W. Kiene, who owned the building at the time, donated it to the Orlando City Council, and since that time, it has been the home of CityArts Orlando as a space for visual and performing arts.

Many local ghost hunters and paranormal investigators agree, however, that not all of the building's former owners and tenants have left. There are regular reports of knocks, creaks, footsteps and other sounds, as well as unexpected cold spots, all of which skeptics might dismiss as normal occurrences within an old building. There have also been numerous reports of floral scents (of which gardenias seem to be the most frequently identified), but again, this could be attributed to someone heavily perfumed having recently passed through the rooms and hallways.

Harder to dismiss are the accounts gathered by author Thomas Cook from dancers during the building's Arthur Murray days, who reported that while they were practicing alone, they had the sudden sense of dancing with an unseen partner. While the second floor was being used as a small movie theater, there were regular reports of lost items showing up in improbable locations days later. There is also the 2002 case of an actress with the Mad Cow Theater Company who found her performance during *The Laramie*

Project disrupted when a police officer escorted an elderly woman directly across the stage. After the show, the actress discovered that she alone among her troupe had witnessed the two others on stage.

Harder still to dismiss are the many sightings of a female apparition (of the "woman in white" variety) who occasionally spends her nights wandering through the halls and art galleries, disrupting activities. She has also been spotted on the stairway between the first and second floor. It is presumed that this is the wife of Gordon Rogers, and some speculate that her presence is her way of posthumously making known her displeasure at the exclusivity of her husband's club for affluent gentlemen.

What of Gordon himself? Though he is spotted less frequently than his wife, he has been seen there as well, sometimes wandering the halls and, at other times, peering out through a second-floor window.

STRANDED AT THE STATION:
CHURCH STREET STATION AND STRAND HOTEL

Prior to 1880, Orlando had grown in fits and starts, evolving gradually from a swamp to a cattle town and then to a citrus producer. The engine that would drive the area's first real boom was the woodfired type attached to the trains that would eventually connect Orlando to the rest of the state and the country. The first such line was built in 1880 by the South Florida Railroad from Tampa to Sanford. One year later, that line was extended to Jacksonville, and from there, it reached the network of other railroads that ran north and south along the East Coast of the United States.

The railroad that ran between Orlando and Tampa was acquired by Henry Plant as part of his Plant System. In 1889, Plant hired contractor T.B. Cotter from Sanford to build the city's third station at Church Street. The Richardsonian Romanesque structure, erected at a cost of $18,000, was opened to the public in 1890 and served the area for thirty-six years until the Sligh Avenue train station opened. This marked the first decline of the Church Street Station, which was reduced to freight operations and then gradually decayed, accumulating dust and tales of hauntings. Bumby Hardware continued to operate next to the depot and was joined in 1924 by Selmon's Department Stores, as well as other retailers under the shadow of the station, which remained unoccupied—at least by the living.

This page: Exterior and interior of the Cheyenne Saloon. *Photographs by the author*.

Like its alleged ghostly residents, however, the station itself was destined for an afterlife, which began in the 1970s. Rosie O'Grady's Good Time Emporium opened in the former Selmon's location as a hub and entrance to multiple connected clubs within the structure. This allowed patrons to "club hop" for one cover price. Another popular attraction there was the Western-style Cheyenne Saloon and Opera House. In the 1980s, Bob Snow spearheaded a comprehensive restoration of the building as part of his Church Street Station. The interior was renovated, the eyebrow dormers on the roof were restored, decorative lighting was added and the resurrected station thrived once more—for a time.

In the 1990s, Walt Disney opened its Pleasure Island club district as a competitor with a more affordable entrance fee, and not even investors like Baltimore Gas and Electric Company, F.F. South and Co. and Lou Pearlman could halt the station's slide back toward the metaphorical grave. It has since risen again (and again), and one could make a compelling case that it is the building's continual triumph over its own demise that makes it so perfectly suited for ghosts.

Prior to 2001, when the property changed ownership, Church Street Station (also known as the Old Orlando Railroad Depot) was popular with a different type of sightseeing visitor: ghost hunters and paranormal investigators. They were attracted to the location for its reputed cold spots, voices, sounds of movement coming from empty rooms and orbs of light captured in photographs and film footage (although, as previously mentioned, such light anomalies have lately fallen out of favor with some of those who seek irrefutable proof of the supernatural). Susan and Madison, two of the ghost ambassadors with American Ghost Adventures, attribute the activity in the building primarily to the spirit of train conductor Ernest Mills. According to the guides, Mills was fixated on playing and gambling on games, especially marbles, to such an extent that trains were sometimes delayed until whatever game he was involved in was completed. Such was the extent of his obsession that it continues even after his death, as evidenced by his moving of objects and attempting to communicate through the use of flashlights and K2 (EMF) meters.

A number of sources have incorrectly placed the Strand Hotel at the same location as either the station or the Cheyenne Saloon (which, not surprisingly, is also said to have its own phantom patrons). According to the historians consulted on the matter, the Strand, which opened its doors in 1922, was located at what was most recently Cevíche restaurant.

This page: Exterior and interior of Cevíche (now permanently closed). *Photographs by the author.*

According to Emilio San Martin, who began his ghost tours there, the Strand Hotel also once served as an unofficial brothel, which explains the sound of crying children, as they were supposedly disposed of to cover up the indiscretions of their affluent fathers. Author and paranormal investigator David W. Whitehead similarly described the Strand Hotel as "a notorious brothel," where "many men lost their lives in fights." White also mentions that the children of the hotel's sex workers are known to haunt the rooms.

In 2005, supernatural activity at the location unexpectedly leapt from tour scripts to news headlines when the owners of Amura Japanese Restaurant, who had moved into the space, claimed it was haunted and made that the basis for breaking their lease. They cited reports by subcontractors of apparitions visibly moving through the space at night. One subcontractor, after removing a floor inside the building, reported seeing "a ghostly bartender and two dancing girls reflected in a mirror" (interesting that this particular claim of seeing ghostly figures in a mirror was repeated later throughout the time that the restaurant Ceviche occupied the space). In an effort to assuage their tenants, the owners offered to perform an exorcism and evict any unwanted (and nonpaying) entities from the space. Eventually, the building's owner sued for $2.6 million to cover a decade of rent and damages while also asking that a judge determine if there are any ghosts in the building.

While the court found no evidence of spooks or specters, some local paranormal investigators and ghost hunters disagree with that assessment. Other frequently recorded experiences at the location include the sounds of a ghostly piano player and a man wearing a top hat wandering one of the hallways near what was the Improv Comedy Club and Restaurant. Numerous visitors have also reported feeling unseen hands pulling at their clothes and hair.

In 2020, citing the impact of COVID-19 on its business, Ceviche, the most recent business at the location, announced that it was permanently closing its doors. Since that time, the space has remained unoccupied—at least by the living. Contractors have been working in the space, though seldom the same crew for very long, one observer noted. Though unsubstantiated, familiar-sounding rumors have started to circulate about human bones being secreted away in the walls of the building, and it's said that the difficulty in retaining teams to complete the renovations has less to do with contract disputes and more to do with strange and uncanny experiences, such as tools suddenly going missing and reappearing in unexpected places, the sound of voices attached to no discernable source, shadows that behave strangely and vanish when approached and other unsettling happenings.

But then, that's all just talk—isn't it?

FOOD AND SPIRITS: HAMBURGER MARY'S

Like Gordon Rogers, Joseph Bumby Sr. arrived in Orlando from Great Britain at a time when the city was still essentially just a tiny Central Florida cow town. He started a profitable business selling grain, hay and fertilizer from a Church Street warehouse. When the railroad arrived, his warehouse became a depot, and he assumed the additional role of ticket agent. By 1886, he had finished building his own store, Bumby Hardware, for which he is best known today. The business remained in his family for the next eighty years, earning it recognition as the longest-running family-held business in Orlando. After the store closed in 1966, the property was acquired by Bob Snow as part of the Church Street Station entertainment complex and designated an Orlando Historic Landmark in 1978.

A number of businesses came and went until 2008, when Hamburger Mary's moved into the space and established itself as a local favorite. The restaurant's dedication to "inclusivity, leadership and true entrepreneurial spirit" recently earned it recognition as City District Main Street's business of the month in February 2023. The spirit of entrepreneurship, however, isn't the only type of spirit that some say can be found there today.

Seasoned ghost hunters have reported light anomalies and cold spots, the inexplicable sounds of someone knocking on the walls, as well as compelling EVP recordings at the location. But it's the little girl in a Victorian dress who steals the show. Multiple eyewitnesses have described her tapping on windows to attract the attention of patrons and then waving to them. She has also been spotted skipping down the street at night. Her carefree nature has led more than a few who've encountered her to speculate that she is either unaware of or unconcerned by her own death.

A second, less frequently seen ghost said to linger at Mary's is a spectral bartender who wipes down the counters. Some who have seen him say that he fit in so naturally, it took them a moment to realize he wasn't an employee wearing a costume. Of course, when he caught their eyes, smiled and dematerialized, they were left with less doubt about his role there.

Possibly taking their cues from the owners and employees, both of these ghosts have been described as playful and happy to be fixtures in the restaurant and part of the Bumby Block's full menu of hauntings.

FASHIONABLY LATE: THE GHOST OF GERTRUDE SWEET

If you've walked along the footpath by the train tracks between West Washington Street and West Church Street, you've more than likely noticed the embossed bronze sign hanging from the red-brick wall. It depicts a stylish-looking young woman with a parasol over her shoulder and the phrase "Gertrude's Walk." The Gertrude for whom the path is named is Gertrude Sweet, who was born on June 17, 1862, in New Orleans and moved to Orlando to join her three siblings in 1875. One of those siblings, Charles D. Sweet, became Orlando's sixth mayor, prior to which he was the surveyor responsible for laying out much of the city's network of streets (which goes a long way toward explaining why Gertrude's name is on both a walkway and an avenue).

Before having her name on landmarks, however, Gertrude was recognized by the *Orlando Sentinel* as "the most beautiful woman in Orange County." In her youth, she was, by all accounts, the belle of every ball, and even though she married, raised a family and passed away in 1945 at the age of eighty-three, it seems that she's not quite ready to relinquish her title.

That, at least, is the way one local ghost tour guide named Heather tells it. She shared the tale of a bride and her entourage who happened to be taking the ghost tour one evening ahead of her wedding. The bride apparently made some disparaging remarks about Gertrude, comparing her beauty unfavorably to her own, and found that the rest of the evening, whenever she crossed Gertrude's Walk, her hair and clothing were pulled, and she was scratched and pushed by an unseen presence. While this was the most extreme example, other young women have similarly and unwittingly found themselves the target of Gertrude's ire.

Of course, more often, Gertrude is said to make her presence known in other, less confrontational ways. In addition to electromagnetic spikes and sudden chills, some believe that the strong scent of the rose perfume Gertrude wore is an indicator that she is nearby.

By all accounts, Gertrude was a proud woman in life and remains so in the afterlife. It's probably best to just be respectful of her dreams of long-faded glory and make no attempt to pry that imaginary tiara from her cold, dead hands.

This page: Gertrude's Walk.
Photographs by the author.

DEAD GONE META: TERROR ON CHURCH STREET

The 1990s saw a number of interesting changes and innovations in the entertainment industry. For one thing, in the world of horror films, "meta" became a thing in 1996 with the release of Wes Craven's first installment in the *Scream* franchise, a scary movie in which survival depends on the protagonists' knowledge of scary movies.

Elsewhere, the idea of scare attractions was being launched. Among the early pioneers was Pasaje del Terror, which originated at a meeting in Argentina and first opened in 1988 in Bilbao, Spain. Based on its overwhelming success, it became a year-round attraction and expanded elsewhere in Europe.

In 1991, the concept leapt the pond and landed in downtown Orlando, as Terror on Church Street (later changed to Terror in the Heart of Orlando, when Church Street Station complained that the font used for "Church Street" too closely resembled its own logo). Anthony Perkins, a horror industry icon and Hitchcock protégé, was selected as the event's spokesperson. Ignacio Brieva served as creative consultant and head of production, and alongside Ed Marzola and Maria de la Roza, previously a director of art and art history at an Orlando high school, he oversaw operations. David Clevinger from the Ice House Theater in Mount Dora came on board as the art director. From top to bottom, the team was a creative production powerhouse.

When Terror on Church Street first opened on November 8, 1991, as a year-round attraction at the corner of Orange Avenue and Church Street inside of what had once been a Woolworth's and Boone's Hardware Store, it filled more than twenty rooms on two floors. Its success spread beyond local enthusiasts to become transformative industrywide. Universal Studios Florida just down the road was paying attention, and it also launched its first Fright Nights at the park as a three-day event. Based on the demand created, in part, by Terror, Universal's event evolved into the season-long programming known today as Halloween Horror Nights.

The reign of Terror in Orlando lasted just six years. By 1998, it was the only tenant still on the block where it began. As local businesses dwindled, foot traffic, the lifeblood for the attraction, dried up as well. It closed on May 2, 1999, and in 2003, the entire structure was demolished and resurrected as CMX Cinemas Plaza Café 12.

A billboard from November 1991 advertising Terror. *Photograph courtesy of the Orlando Regional History Center/ Orlando Sentinel Collection.*

More than a few of the individuals who were consulted while researching this book waxed nostalgic whenever conversation touched on Terror. But it lives on as a local legend for reasons beyond it being a scare industry upstart and trendsetter. It was also part of that 1990s zeitgeist mentioned earlier: meta. What, after all, could possibly be more meta than a haunted attraction that is actually haunted?

That, at least, is what several individuals who visited or worked at the attraction claim. Among those who claim that the attraction was truly haunted is self-titled "paranormal paparazzi" Michael Gavin, who began his journey into the supernatural while working there (and subsequently at the short-lived Skull Kingdom). Among the tales to which he can attest is that of the animatronic clown named Zelda that continued to move on its own, even after its electricity was turned off, and how the attraction's effects in the attic malfunctioned one night after one of the employees used a Ouija board.

Another source who worked there shared an experience he had after the attraction closed one day. He and another coworker noticed a man and woman wandering through one of the rooms. Thinking that they were either scare actors or mischievous visitors who had been hiding until after the attraction closed, he followed them in, only to watch them both walk right through a solid wall.

Still shot from a Terror on Church Street promotional video. *Public domain.*

There is the story of two children who died in the building during a fire. Following complaints by guests who saw small children running through the attraction, management investigated but found no trace of them. The site also relates the tale of a strange mist turning into the face of a man, which was captured on surveillance video.

As of yet, there have been no further reports of ghostly activity at the new entertainment complex, which leads one to wonder: Was the haunted attraction really haunted, or were these stories concocted as clever marketing schemes designed to pump life back into a dying business? Given that it's unlikely we'll ever get a definitive answer, maybe it's better to ask: What would you like to believe?

AN APPETITE FOR THE PARANORMAL: THE KRESS BUILDING

Before becoming the upscale Kress Chophouse, from 1936 to 1975, the Kress building at 15 West Church Street was home to one of the S.H. Kress and Company's chain of department stores. The L-shaped, Art Deco–style building composed of masonry over steel-reinforced concrete was erected in 1930 by the G.A. Miller Company. It featured terra-cotta ornamentation of parrots looking in through its windows from the ledges where they're perched and other details that were added by Edward F. Sibbert. Three years after Kress vacated the eponymous building, it was added to the list of Orlando Historic Landmarks and was occupied for a time by the dinner attraction King Henry's Feast.

Exterior of the Kress building.
Photograph by the author.

Today, the Kress building is as popular with those looking for a steak dinner as it is among those with a taste for local history and ghosts. Visitors and employees have reported activity here of both the seen and unseen varieties, ranging from the sound of footsteps after hours, when the building is empty, to the appearance of apparitions.

Madison, a ghost ambassador with American Ghost Adventures, interviewed staff at the restaurant. During the interview, multiple employees confirmed they'd had experiences they could not explain. These included not only unexplained drafts and cold spots but also the overwhelming feeling of another presence when they were alone and clearly hearing the restaurant's general manager calling out for them, even when the manager was nowhere in or near the building.

According to Madison, this mimicry behavior, in which a spirit assumes the voice or shape of another living being, is a potential sign of something more sinister than mere playfulness. She suggests that any sentient creature, living or dead, that attempts to deceive another should be regarded with a healthy amount of caution.

WHO'S WHO AND WHAT'S THAT?: GREENWOOD CEMETERY

In 1880, with a population of two hundred, Orlando might not have officially been a city yet, but that was all about to change with the arrival of the railroad. Correctly anticipating one of the essential needs of a community about to undergo rapid growth, eight individuals purchased twenty-six acres of land from John W. Anderson for $1,000, thereby establishing Orlando Cemetery and giving the nascent city its first public burial ground. (In case you're wondering, those eight buyers were W.R. Anno, C.A. Boone, James Delaney, James K. Duke, J.H. Livingston, Nat Poyntz, Samuel A. Robinson and I.P. Wescott.)

Grave of Baseball Hall of Famer Joe Tinker. *Photograph by the author.*

Control of the cemetery was turned over to the city in 1892, following a fire the previous year that destroyed many of the cemetery's original wooden headstones. Along with the new owners, in 1915, there came a new name, Greenwood Cemetery, by which the cemetery has been known ever since. The city also expanded the cemetery multiple times to keep pace with its own growth. Today, Greenwood Cemetery sits on ninety-two acres (excluding the eighteen and a half acres that make up Greenwood Wetlands Park).

It should be made clear that just because Greenwood was a "public cemetery," this doesn't necessarily mean that it was open to everyone— just to everyone who could afford it. Hence, the list of its eternal residents reads like a who's who of Orlando's leading families, including no less than eight of the city's mayors (Boone, Palmer, Gore, Bryan, Parramore, Smith, Beacham, Langford and Beardall); T.G. Lee (the founder of the eponymous dairy business); Joseph Bumby (of local hardware fame); Orlando's first undertaker, Edgar Richards; funeral home owner Carey Hand; civil rights activist July Perry; the Eppes and Shine families, descended from President Thomas Jefferson (Francis Wayle Eppes VII was his grandson); and Baseball Hall of Famer Joe Tinker. There are also sections dedicated to the Black victims of the Ocoee Masacre and the more recent Pulse Nightclub shooting.

Predictably, since Greenwood is the city's oldest and largest cemetery, there are also plenty of urban legends and eyewitness accounts of otherworldly activity (admittedly, the two are sometimes difficult to untangle and distinguish from each other). The following are a few of those ghosts that are most frequently encountered.

THE GHOST OF FRED WEEKS

Is there anything, according to legends and literature, more likely to spawn a ghost than a grudge held so tightly that it persists even after the holder has expired? Such, it's claimed, is the case with affluent businessman Fred Weeks, who, like many such northerners, decided to purchase a piece of investment property in Orlando. Being of English stock, he decided to buy from three other English remittance men but discovered shortly thereafter that he'd been swindled—the land he was sold turned out to be worthless swampland. While Fred was hardly the first or the last to fall victim to a Florida real estate scam, he was among the angriest about it and almost certainly the most creative as far as how he chose to exhibit that anger. Specifically, he bought a plot near the front gates of Greenwood Cemetery, built a mausoleum and had a biblical quote inscribed on it. The passage from Luke 10:30 reads, "A certain man went down from Jerusalem to Jericho and fell among thieves." Below the quote, he added the names of the three men who had scammed him. Making known the identities and dubious characters of those who conned him had the desired effect; he was refunded his investment, and the three men also purchased his cemetery plot to remove the message that implicated them.

Left and opposite: Fred Weeks's mausoleum and detail of the inscription on the door. *Photographs by the author.*

That might have been the end of the story, but apparently, old Fred wasn't entirely satisfied that the three thieves had learned their lesson. In the later part of the 1910s, he bought another plot roughly one hundred feet from his first. This time, on the front of the tomb, he included the verse from the Bible but left a blank space beneath it. One might suppose he did this to let the three swindlers know he was keeping an eye on them (or that the lawsuits they threatened him with kept him from once again naming names or that the families of these men had the names removed—accounts vary). Weeks was eventually laid to rest (at least temporarily) in this second mausoleum, which he has all to himself. After his death, his wife took their children and headed for the less litigious if not greener pastures of Indiana. According to some, however, Fred is still in the grips of his gripe as an earthbound spirit seen standing in front of or nearby his eternal monument.

GHOSTS OF THE CIVIL WAR

The division between Union and Confederate soldiers persists in death at Greenwood Cemetery, where separate sections are designated for soldiers who fought in the blue uniform of the North and those from the South who were clad in gray. According to multiple investigators, it is the Confederate spirits that seem most prone to roam among the oak trees and interact with the living. During a visit in 2013 by Greg Bush and Mary Jo Fister of Offthetrails Paranormal Investigations, the couple claim they made contact with two of these spirits who soldier on in the afterlife. Although the team had a variety of technologies with them (including full-spectrum and still cameras, K2 meters, EVP recorders, MEL meters and a ghost box recorder, also known as an Ovilus), it was the relatively rudimentary flashlight through which the spirits chose to communicate, indicating the answers to yes or no questions by either turning the light on (for yes) or off (for no). Using this method, the team discovered that one of the soldiers originally hailed from Georgia, while the other called Tennessee home in life. One of these two was an infantryman, and the other was a lieutenant.

While it is unclear what keeps these Confederate soldiers from a peaceful slumber, what is clear is that they share the cemetery with soldiers from a number of other conflicts, including the Spanish-American War, World War I, World War II, the Korean War and the Vietnam War. Could it be that they feel slighted seeing the respect paid to those who fought in other conflicts? Bring a spirit box, a flashlight and EVP recorders, and maybe you can find the elusive answer for yourself.

THE WILMOTT MAUSOLEUM

The appearance of ghostly soldiers within the cemetery is not confined to the areas designated specifically for veterans of specific wars and conflicts. One, in fact, has been spotted somewhat regularly in front of the Wilmott family mausoleum. The mausoleum is one of only two such structures in the cemetery (the other belonging to Fred Weeks, who was discussed earlier in this section). In keeping with the Wilmott family's position of prominence in Orlando society circa 1900, this eternal resting place is situated atop the highest point in the cemetery.

Wealth and power, however, do not preclude tragedy, which struck the Wilmotts when their grandson Fred Wilmott Jr. and his friend Frank Pounds Jr. drowned at a local swimming hole. Both boys were just five years old at the time and supposedly misjudged the depth of the water.

Interestingly, neither of the two boys are known to make posthumous appearances at the place where Fred and his family's remains are kept. Rather, it is an older man who is most often seen at the entrance of the mausoleum, wearing an antiquated military uniform and staring off into the distance. Was he a brother, cousin or some other relation of Fred Jr.'s? Or does this apparition visit the family resting place for other reasons?

BABY LAND

While there's no denying that the death of two five-year-old boys is tragic, these boys are neither the only children nor the youngest who have been laid to rest at Greenwood Cemetery. In fact, there's an entire section of the cemetery known as Baby Land (which is further divided into Baby Land 1, 2 and 3), the resting place for children five years old and younger. More than a few of the markers here have only one date, indicating both birth and death. While paranormal activity in all three of these sections is said to be extremely high, Baby Lands 1 and 3 are especially active. Multiple visitors and investigators have reported the sounds of laughter, cries and children

Baby Land 3. *Photograph by the author.*

playing, as well as what sounds like a faint tune from a toy music box. Another frequently reported experience from this section of the cemetery is the sensation of a tug on clothing, often below the waist, very much like the hand of a small child trying to get the attention of an adult.

Some have suggested that the spirits of the children are not alone here. Renowned cryptid hunter and author Mark Muncy referenced another presence said to haunt this area, "a mysterious lady in white with a dark face and glowing, red eyes. She is often seen through a ray of moonlight as she walks past the grave markers in Baby Land 3."

Greenwood Cemetery has plenty of other stories to tell, like the tale of those who came to rest there by way of Sunland Hospital (see page 59), for those who are willing and able to listen. Whether one is seeking history or haunts, Greenwood provides a window and, some whisper, a doorway into the past. Those seeking to find out more and potentially have a firsthand experience with one or more of the cemetery's famous residents should check for an upcoming guided moonlight walking tour of the grounds.

HIDDEN HANDS: THE CAREY HAND FUNERAL HOME

Around 1885, at about the same time Orlando's first public cemetery was being established, Elijah Hand moved to the area and brought with him, as the city's first embalmer, an innovation that would have a related and equally far-reaching impact. Prior to embalming, the deceased were typically buried within twenty-four hours. Those who passed away in the morning were usually buried that afternoon, and those who died in the night were buried the following morning.

Hand, as Orlando's first embalmer, forged a logical and, by all accounts, productive partnership with Edgar A. Richards, who served as the city's first undertaker. The dawning of the 1890s, however, found Richards approaching his twilight years. He retired, and Hand continued the business on his own.

Ever the entrepreneur, Hand was anything but idle, and given his training in carpentry, in 1905, he opened a storefront at 15–17 West Pine Street, combining furniture making with funeral services. If those two skill sets seem oddly incongruous, at the time, being versed in both trades made good money as well as good sense, since those in the funeral business were often required to construct coffins for their customers. It has been suggested by some that Hand also took the opportunity to cross-market his skills; since embalming allowed bodies to be preserved longer than ever before, he could display them at repose in the furniture he had built. This particular tale is most likely (but not certainly) apocryphal.

The preservation of bodies, thanks to embalming, also meant that friends and family members of the deceased who lived farther away would have enough time to travel and attend funerals, and that, in turn, meant that they needed places to stay. Once again, Elijah Hand saw an opportunity and converted some of the rooms on the second floor of his shop for lodgers.

In 1907, a second set of hands joined the business when Elijah brought in his son Carey, who was also trained in embalming. Seven years later, Carey Hand took over the business and built a funeral home of his own at 36 West Pine Street, directly across the street from the one his father had operated. Continuing not only the family business but also an interest in innovation, the Carey Hand Funeral Home became the first in Orlando to have its own chapel. Then in 1925, it became the first funeral home in the South to have its own crematorium (a feature that was used by Daniel L. Dewey, the inventor of the Dewey Decimal System, as part of his final arrangements).

Exterior of what was once Elijah Hand's furniture store. *Photograph by the author*.

Opposite: Exterior of the former Carey Hand Funeral Home and historical marker. *Photographs by the author*.

Fast forward to the present day. The funeral company has again changed hands (while retaining the name, Hand) and now goes by the name Carey Hand Colonial Funeral Home. It's changed its location as well, now situated along the northern edge of the Lake Terrace neighborhood. The funeral home that Carey Hand established on Pine Street is now owned by UCF as part of its downtown campus. Across the street, the two-story structure that served as the original furniture store and funeral parlor has seen so many different uses over the years, it's almost impossible to keep track of them. A short list of business occupants includes a daycare center, a school and a slew of bars and nightclubs (of which the Blue Room, Déjà vu, Club Zen, Liquid Night Club, Voyage Night Club and Ice Orlando are just a few). More recently, a marketing firm moved into the space and shared a wall with the appropriately situated Cocktails and Screams, a Halloween- and horror-themed bar. With all of these changes and renovations over time, is it really any surprise that more than dust and plaster are said to have been disturbed?

CAREY HAND FUNERAL HOME

36 WEST PINE STREET

CAREY HAND CAME TO ORLANDO IN 1907 AND BOUGHT HIS FATHER'S EMBALMING BUSINESS IN 1914. HE OPENED THIS FUNERAL HOME IN 1920, DESIGNED BY ARCHITECT F.H. TRIMBLE IN THE TUSCAN STYLE WITH A CHAPEL, THE FIRST OF ITS KIND IN FLORIDA. THE CREMATORIUM, BUILT IN 1925, WAS THE FIRST IN THE ENTIRE SOUTH. THE CAREY HAND FUNERAL HOME OPERATED HERE UNTIL 1987.

PLAQUE SPONSORED BY
THE ORLANDO COMMUNITY REDEVELOPMENT AGENCY

Michael Gavin, a self-described paranormal paparazzi who has written for *GHOST!* magazine and co-produced Orlando Hauntings Ghost Tours back in 2000, explained in an *Orlando Weekly* article that most of the reported activity at 17 West Pine Street comes from the second floor of the building. Numerous visitors have heard phantom footsteps, felt cold spots and experienced powerful feelings of uneasiness and dread there. During some of the building's previous nightclub incarnations, its second floor served as a green room, where performers would wait to take the stage. Several of them complained that the air seemed oppressively thick and heavy in the room. Apparitions of a woman and small children have been spotted running through the halls.

At one point, a psychic who was filming a segment for a cable TV program had encounters of her own on the second floor of the building. She claimed she came into contact with multiple spirits, one of which went by the name Robert. That name comes up again in an experience related by a former employee of one of the nightclubs at the location. This individual had befriended the young son of one of the club owners, and the boy would run to greet her whenever she called for him. One day, however, she called his name but got no answer. After a few attempts to summon him, she became concerned and went up to the second floor, where she peeked into the various rooms that had been converted into offices. At length, she found him sitting cross-legged on the floor of one of the rooms with a strangely devilish grin on his face. After the woman plied the boy with questions, he finally relented and confessed that he had been "just playing" with his imaginary friend Mr. Robert. The boy was banned from playing on the second floor after that incident, but what of his unseen companion? Could it be the same Robert the psychic encountered?

Madison and Susie of American Ghost Adventures added that it isn't just inside the pair of Hand buildings where ghosts have been encountered; they have also shown themselves in the street between the two. Numerous visitors who have gone walking there at night have heard the unmistakable clopping of horses' hooves. These sounds are suspected of being temporal reverberations from the horses that once carried Orlando's residents to their final destinations.

THE LADY OF LAKE LUCERNE

Sightings of female apparitions wearing long white gowns or dresses are sufficiently common worldwide to earn them their own category as "women in white" or "white ladies." In medieval legends, their appearances, like those of a banshee, are considered portents of impending death, while elsewhere, their appearances have been attributed to a vast array of generally tragic circumstances, including but not limited to an unrequited love that outlasts life itself, an accidental death, a murder, a death during childbirth, a death by suicide, the act of an unfaithful spouse and, not infrequently, some combination of these.

Just as there can be many variants on the specific type of ghost known as the woman in white, so, too, can one specific ghost of that type show up in a variety of slightly different sightings. Such is the case with the white lady said to haunt Lake Lucerne.

The first and most frequently described encounter occurs near an old oak tree along South Orange Avenue. The incorporeal woman is said to wander the area after dark, only to suddenly disappear once she passes the oak. Mark Muncy related a slightly different version of the story, in which the lady shows up on moonlit nights over the water itself and appears to descend the stairway of an invisible boat.

One final and more recent story involving the lady of Lake Lucerne was told by a woman who was working at a retirement home across from the lake when she spotted the lady in white walking past the building. A security guard was entering the building at about the same time, and, concerned that perhaps a resident had gotten locked out, the observer asked him if he saw the lady outside. The guard immediately ran back outside but found no one else on the street or sidewalk outside.

As no one has reported having a conversation with the woman, it's anyone's guess as to what keeps her wandering around the lake. Perhaps, as one paranormal investigator said in jest, she's looking for her lost ghost dog. Of course, if that's the case, she might be looking at the wrong lake (see the story of ghost dog in the following section).

THE GHOST DOG OF LAKE EOLA

Do ghosts have to have once been human beings, or are other living creatures also able to return from the other side? Many late-night visitors to Lake Eola

Lake Eola. *Photograph by the author.*

have shared personal experiences that caused them to reconsider their own narrowly defined ideas of spirits. Specifically, we're referring to the ghost dog of Lake Eola, described as a small brown terrier most often seen along the eastern side of the lake. Over the last several years, there have been frequent accounts of the dog appearing suddenly, running and playing with humans and other canines and then vanishing abruptly. As of this time, neither a name nor a backstory has been determined for the dog. Some have posited that the dog drowned in the lake, either by accident or at the hands of a cruel owner, but however the canine arrived in its spectral form, death has apparently done nothing to diminish its playful nature.

BANGERS AND MAX: THE HARP AND CELT IRISH PUB AND RESTAURANT

Celtic folklore abounds with tales of spirits and ghosts, including death omen spirits like the banshee, whose wail foretells of a death in one's family, and the headless horseman, called the Dullahan, who cradles his own head in the crook of his arm and recites the names of all those soon to perish while lashing his horse not with a whip but with a human spinal column. Of course, you're not likely to encounter anything quite so terrifying at the popular family-owned Harp and Celt bar and restaurant situated on South Magnolia Avenue, which was opened in 2007.

Like the nearby building on Church Street, where the restaurant Cevíche was located, this address is alleged to have had a long and sordid past as a local brothel. While such claims are often difficult if not impossible to prove, given the liminal nature of such enterprises, there does seem to be someone

Exterior of the Harp and Celt and the interior of the smaller room where most of the ghostly activity takes place. *Photographs by the author.*

lingering at the site who takes an interest in women. That, according to Ting Rappa and her team at American Ghost Adventures, is the spirit named Maximilian. Though he bristles over being called Max, Rappa believes that he is more of a protective spirit and sees his role as a caretaker at the restaurant. His apparition has been seen in the corner of the smaller room inside the building.

2
East and West of Downtown Orlando

BRICK AND MORTEM: THE GHOSTS OF COLONIAL PLAZA

The idea of the undead roaming a mall might seem peculiar to anyone who hasn't seen George Romero's *Dawn of the Dead* or the more recent remake. Of course, in the movies, it was zombies, shambling, reanimated corpses, rather than ghosts that roamed the shopping complex. But whether it's a fictional location or the very real vestiges of Orlando's Colonial Plaza, the underlying rationale seems to hold up: the unliving continue to go to those places and perform the same activities they did when they were alive.

When it was built in 1957, Colonial Plaza was a big deal. It was the very first enclosed mall in Central Florida, which evolved from a strip mall in the part of town known as the Milk District (named for the T.G. Lee Dairy, which had been based there since the 1920s). President Lyndon Johnson paid the mall a visit in 1967, and for a time, the mall thrived. By the 1980s, however, the mall had fallen on hard times, as other shopping centers and big-box stores drew customers away. Not even a major renovation in 1983 could turn the tide, and by the 1990s, many of the stores were vacant. It didn't help matters that to get from one end of the mall to the other, shoppers had to pass through the cavernous, empty space that had once been Jordan Marsh.

Most of the mall fell to the wrecking ball in 1995, save for just two former stores, a Walgreens and what, at the time, was the Belk-Lindsey department store (now a Floor & Decor located at 3113 East Colonial Drive).

This page: Exterior and interior of the Floor & Decor, which used to be part of Colonial Plaza. *Photographs by the author.*

Author Thomas Cook documents the lore related to these Colonial Plaza remnants. The legend related to him about the Belk-Lindsey was that on the day it was slated to be torn down, a demolition supervisor made one final walk-through. He emerged from the store pale and trembling. When asked what happened, he told his staff that voices in the building had pleaded with him to spare their home. (The exact and somewhat ironic phrasing, according to Cook, was that "they wouldn't have anywhere else to 'live.'") Whether the request of the disembodied voices was the deciding factor or not, that part of the building did in fact survive unscathed.

The other surviving portion of the former mall is the Walgreens at 2420 East Colonial Drive. On the second floor of the building, which was a cafeteria, employees received "gifts" from time to time (including an unmarked greeting card, pencils and other small trinkets), which they believed came from their resident ghost. The temperature was said to fluctuate significantly in the stairwell. On two occasions, the store was visited by a shadow figure. The first time, it entered through the front of the store and left a few minutes later, triggering the antitheft alarm. The second time, when it left, all of the power in the building went out briefly. Once the power was restored, a manager noticed that the point-of-sale system display said, "store closed," which was unusual, as that particular Walgreens was open twenty-four hours a day and, for that reason, had never had the "closed" status programmed into the system. Additional unexplained phenomena included automatic doors opening and closing on their own and merchandise inexplicably being thrown from shelves.

GROUNDED: ORLANDO EXECUTIVE AIRPORT

Even if you're not someone who suffers from aerophobia (the fear of flying), airports can be stressful places. Between worrying about delays, lost luggage, crowded spaces and a host of other challenges, it's not all that surprising that some choose to avoid Orlando International Airport and opt for the smaller Orlando Executive Airport near the State Road 408 East–West Expressway instead.

Of course, this particular airport might give some travelers something else to be concerned about, specifically late at night, when visitors have reported the strong scent of cigar smoke emanating from the western part of the airport and have heard disembodied voices and conversations taking place in a foreign language.

Aerial image of Orlando Executive Airport, taken in February 1999. *Wikimedia Commons*.

If that language happens to be Italian or German, there might be a historical connection. In 1940, the United States Army Air Corps took control of the airport (then known as Orlando Municipal Airport) for use first by the I Bomber Command and subsequently by the Army Air Forces Antisubmarine Command (AAFAC), which flew patrols along both of Florida's coasts. After the United States entered World War II in December 1941, the Orlando Army Air Base came to serve another function, housing as many as six hundred prisoners of war who had been captured from the German Afrika Korps and later from Allied campaigns in France and Italy. In accordance with the rules regarding POWs detailed in the 1929 Geneva Convention, the prisoners' accommodations and meals had to be on par with those of American soldiers. Additionally, under supervision, many of these prisoners worked at citrus farms, garages and a variety of other local businesses, earning roughly one dollar a day. Despite receiving fair treatment, some of the prisoners died while being held there, and of those, it seems, a few never caught their connection to the next world.

There are scattered reports that, in addition to the ghosts of the POWs, a spectral guard dog also prowls the area. If disturbed, it will give chase, but it will ultimately vanish before it can sink its teeth into any mortal flesh.

Ghost dog excepted, most of the spirits at the airport who are awaiting their departure seem far more focused on making conversation with each other than bothering the living.

STAINS THAT TIME WON'T WASH AWAY: THE FORMER SITE OF THE SUNLAND MENTAL HOSPITAL

The overwhelming majority of haunted locations in and around the City Beautiful are harmless in nature. Some fall into the category of "residual hauntings," or "death echoes," in which the spirits seem to be caught in a loop like a projection, unaware of the presence of any living spectators.

Other more interactive, or "intelligent," hauntings feature spirits that exhibit the full range of personalities and emotions from playful, helpful and curious to grumpy, frustrated and even seething with rage. But one place above all others in the Orlando area is consistently referred to as exuding a palpable negative energy that is deeply disturbing, malevolent and sometimes just downright evil.

Almost without fail, these descriptions are of the former site of the Sunland Mental Hospital, where countless young patients met with unspeakable cruelty and abuse while they were kept in dangerously unsanitary living conditions. All that remains of the institution is a gradually decaying portion of the administrative building, which stands incongruously next to a playground. However, even that small remnant of the facility is enough to give visitors shudders, especially those familiar with the hospital's soiled and sordid history.

Of course, the hospital didn't start out under a black cloud—quite the opposite, in fact. It began with the very best of intentions. Before it achieved infamy under the name for which it's best known, Sunland Hospital was first opened in 1952 as one in a chain of twelve W.T. Edwards Tuberculosis Hospitals throughout the state of Florida. Named for the Virginian who came to Florida in 1925 and served as the first chairman of the State Tuberculosis Board, the admirable aim of these facilities was to isolate and treat patients for tuberculosis (TB).

The buildings all followed a similar design, long, thin structures consisting of five floors, with multiple windows to allow ample fresh air, which was thought to be the best treatment at the time for TB. Less than a decade later, however, the discovery of a vaccine made such hospitals obsolete, and they were closed. Control of the buildings was passed to the Florida Department of Health, which reopened the facilities as Sunland Training Centers. (The Orlando facility was an exception, as it was the only one not housed in a former W.T. Edwards Hospital.)

Under new management and a new name, these facilities cared for the most physically, mentally and emotionally disabled children and adults. Over the next ten years, funding dwindled and led to understaffing, a lack of training and worse. When a formal investigation was eventually conducted in the 1970s, it revealed what can only be described as atrocities: unsafe surgical areas, roach infestations, rodent bites and beatings. More than four hundred patients had been force-fed a thick gruel three times a day through gastric feeding tubes. Lobotomies, electric shock therapy and heavy sedation were all methods the facilities regularly employed.

Promised reforms were never implemented, and the Association of Retarded Citizens (ARC) filed a federal class-action lawsuit for gross neglect and abuse. The facilities were closed in 1983, but it was far too late for the patients who suffered lifelong ailments, injuries and deformities (including a variety of infections, nutritional deficiencies and dermatological conditions) as a result of their time at Sunland.

In 1983, the State of Florida closed all Sunland facilities. Given the horrors that had transpired at what has been described as a hell for both patients and staff, stories of hauntings began leaking like shadows from the looming abandoned building. Naturally, this appealed to a different crowd, specifically ghost hunters and urban explorers, with tragic consequences.

On July 28, 1997, a new urban legend was born: a twenty-three-year-old who was playing with friends among the ruined buildings fell to his death in an elevator shaft. (A piece that is sometimes added to the story is that, as emergency responders were making their way to the scene, a second call came in from a sheriff's deputy, who indicated that he'd seen a young boy looking out from behind a window on the building's second story.) Author Thomas Cook and others have since amended this legend, identifying the twenty-three-year-old as Keith Murdock and confirming that there was second call but that it came from one of Keith's friends when emergency responders had difficulty locating the young man. Once found, Murdock was transported to a nearby hospital, where, contrary to local lore and despite skull fractures and permanent spinal injuries, he recovered and actually survived the ordeal.

Following the accident and hoping to avert any further incidents, the community lobbied to have the facility demolished. In 1998, the main building was leveled, leaving just the old red-brick administrative building. Today, the place where the mental hospital once stood is a playground. Thus ended a dark and painful chapter in the city's history, but some are convinced that an epilogue to the story is still being penned from beyond the grave.

A complete catalog of paranormal activity reported from this location could likely fill an entire book on its own. In researching the site, David Whitehead gathered multiple firsthand accounts of faces peering out from windows, slamming doors, unexplained flashes of light and throngs of shadow figures lurking throughout the property. He writes of having witnessed luminous orbs, cold spots, EVPs and spikes on his EMF meter, all of which occurred even during the day.

Among the other phenomenon documented at the site are unusual mists and ribbons of energy captured on film, especially at night on the playground, where ghostly apparitions of children have been spotted and the swings sometimes move without any discernable wind. The sounds of children crying have also been frequently reported, and if that seems to echo the wails heard from parts of Greenwood Cemetery (page 47), that might not be coincidental. The patients who perished at Sunland were laid to rest in those allegedly haunted Baby Land sections of Greenwood.

Ultimately, however, whether there are any sentient spirits still bound to the area by their earthly pains, there is a different sort of shadow that hangs over the former facility, that of the terrible wrongs done to one of the most vulnerable segments of society, and that should be more than terrifying enough for even the most hardened ghost seeker.

3

SOUTH OF DOWNTOWN AND INTERNATIONAL DRIVE

SOUTH OF DOWNTOWN

Some immediately recognizable features of the area south of downtown—and throughout Orlando, for that matter—are all the lakes. In fact, the city has over one hundred of them. The largest of these is Lake Harris, which spans 13,788 acres and reaches a depth of thirty feet. The newest is Lake Rose, which was created from a sinkhole that opened in 1981.

These lakes are significant not only in terms of all the waterfront property they create but also because of the long-held connection between ghosts and bodies of water. This goes all the way back to Greek mythology, in which the souls of the dead are carried to the Underworld via the River Styx. In modern times, we recognize water as a conductor of electricity, which has led many paranormal researchers to theorize that ghosts may be able to draw energy more easily from water. Many claim this explains why a large number of hauntings seem to occur near rivers and lakes. Given that Orlando has over one hundred lakes to choose from, it should come as no surprise to learn that some of these natural and man-made bodies of water are apparently every bit as popular among ghosts as they are with the area's living residents.

GHOST WRITER: SIOUX VILLA

Mahlon Gore, born in Climax, Michigan, in 1837, was many things, including a Union soldier during the Civil War, a businessman and newspaper owner, the thirteenth mayor of the city of Orlando (elected to three consecutive terms), the Orlando Board of Trade's first secretary and one of the founders of the First Unitarian Church of Orlando. More than a few Orlando residents, sensitives and spirit hunters have suggested that he might also deserve credit for serving another role since departing this world on June 27, 1916—that of ghost haunting his former abode.

Gore arrived in the Orlando area in the 1880s. Equipped with experience, having previously owned a newspaper in the town of Vermillion, he acquired the *Orange County Reporter*, a two-page weekly publication that was Orlando's sole local paper at the time. Over the next decade, he successfully grew the paper, despite challenges, not least of which was coming back from the brink of ruin in the aftermath of the 1884 fire, which destroyed more than a dozen businesses.

After salvaging his newspaper business, Gore later sold it and went into the real estate business with former Florida governor Sinclair and invested

Exterior of Sioux Villa. *Photograph by the author.*

in orange groves. He also built the first home in a new subdivision on a road that became Gore Avenue, but having a street named after him wasn't enough of a reason to keep his residence there. In 1906, Gore and his wife, Caroline, moved one final time to the home they built on the north side of Lake Lucerne. They named it Sioux Villa after Sioux Falls, Iowa, where Gore had lived for a time. It was here at Sioux Villa that Gore died on June 27, 1916. Given Gore's impact on Orlando, both city hall and the fire department were draped in mourning for a full thirty days after his passing.

Someone at Sioux Villa, however, must have had some unfinished business. Since at least the 1980s, other owners of the home have heard strange noises coming from the attic dormer where Gore once kept a writing desk. Items on the desk were said to have moved, and from time to time, an apparition appeared there as well. Presumably, this has continued since the home was relocated in the 1990s to its present address at 60 Waverly Place, where it now has waterfront access to Lake Copeland.

Most believe that the ghost belongs to either Mahlon Gore or his wife, Caroline, but a few have suggested it could instead be the spirit of a family friend, Frank Sperry, with whom Gore helped realize the First Unitarian Church of Orlando. Like Gore, Sperry served as one of Orlando's mayors and was in office when he passed.

It is not clear precisely who is attempting to pen some final words in the home or what those words may be, but if you're willing to invest in finding the answer for yourself, you can check with a realtor. As of January 2023, the home was back on the market with an asking price of $1,297,777.

UNNAMED AND UNCLAIMED: ORANGE HILL CEMETERY

If the roster of those resting eternally at Greenview Cemetery reads like a who's who of Orlando's history, the list of those resting in Orange Hill Cemetery represents more of a "who knows?" Such, of course, is commonly the case with potters' fields (also known as paupers' cemeteries), where the poor were laid to rest, often without the means to leave behind any stone monument or even a name. In 1901, Orange County purchased forty acres around what today is 1700 East Michigan Street. Today, most visitors would pass it by without a second thought, assuming it to be an empty field, but between 1907 and 1961, it was filled with an estimated 522 graves. The first and oldest known burial there was that of Richard Johnson, "who died

Orange Hill Cemetery in Orlando. *Photograph by the author.*

of 'insanity' at the county jail on May 8, 1907." Today, only five markers remain (dated to the early 1940s), but according to an article from the Orange County Regional History Center (which is said to have ghosts of its own—see page 16), someone or something at Orange Hill is doing its best to ensure that the dead are not forgotten.

For years, locals had been using the grassy area at Fern Creek Avenue and Michigan Street as a park, even though some of them reported feeling uncomfortable there, as if they were being watched. Stories began to circulate about strange happenings there, including one story about a figure cloaked in shadow, yet without any discernable eyes or other facial features, watching and glaring at passersby. In 1997, the Orange County Historical Society undertook the task of properly maintaining the cemetery, thereafter erecting a marker and planting greenery, but according to some, such efforts have not been enough to appease the dead who had been ignored for decades. If you listen carefully, perhaps you can discern the reason from the whispers that are alleged to swirl like a chill wind around this location. Is it the incoherent rambling of Robert Johnson, consumed even in death by madness, or is he perhaps trying to correct the record and convey a different cause of death than the one listed by the old county jail? Or is it one of the other many unnamed dead responsible for the rustling noises and even the occasional scratch or bruise on the ankle or calf of a passerby? Then again, maybe it's just the wind and an overactive imagination.

LAKE CONWAY AND THE GHOST OF MOSES BARBER JR.

Orlando looked a lot different back in 1860s, long before the arrival of the first amusement park, before the rise and fall of the citrus industry, before there were even paved roads. Consequently, crime looked different as well, the theft of cattle being one of the most common offenses. (There wasn't, after all, very much else worth stealing at the time.) Two families in particular, the Mizells and the Barbers, had long-running disputes over the matter.

David Mizell and Moses Barber were both the heads of their own cattle businesses, which provided the Confederate army with beef. After the Civil War, David Mizell became the sheriff and tax collector for Orange County. Moses Barber on the other hand, refused to give up the lost cause of the Confederacy. Unlike Mizell, whom Barber considered a traitorous carpetbagger, Barber refused to pay taxes and support the Reconstruction government. So, Mizell made off with some of Barber's cattle as compensation.

Barber took none too kindly to this and confronted George Bass, a close friend of the Mizell family, essentially wanting to know, "Where's the beef?" David Mizell responded by charging Barber with the "false imprisonment" of Bass, and thus, Barber found an entirely new sort of beef with Mizell, who filed further charges, including arson, polygamy and tax evasion.

Barber had reached the end of his short fuse and informed Mizell that there would be blood if he set foot on his land again. Still, David Mizell, along with his brother Morgan and son Will, crossed over Bull Creek onto Barber's property. David Mizell was ambushed and shot multiple times.

Thus began a feud that ultimately claimed seven lives, despite Mizell's dying wish that his family refrain from spilling more blood trying to avenge his murder.

John Randolf Mizell, the brother of the slain lawman, was the first judge of Orange County, to which he unofficially added the titles of jury and executioner. His demands for swift justice resulted in the deaths of Moses Barber's sons Isaac, who was shot while fleeing arrest, and Moses Jr., who was drowned in Lake Conway. Also killed were William Yates and Lyell Padgett, both friends of the Barber family, and William Bronson, who was a friend of the Mizells.

While most of these individuals seem to have crossed over to whatever awaited them, Moses Jr. apparently inherited his father's stubborn refusal to let things go. Or is it the manner of his demise that kept him earthbound?

This page: The Mizell family graveyard on the grounds of Leu Gardens. *Photographs by the author.*

According to one version of the story, he was tracked down by a posse of three lawmen (Jack Evans, Joe Moody and Bill Duffield) who made camp just south of Lake Conway. Moses Jr. was put in irons to prevent him from escaping, but even his new metal ankle bracelets couldn't stop him. The following morning, the three men tracked Barber to where he had drowned near the shore.

There is, however, an alternate ending written in precisely the sort of cold blood that tends to give rise to tales of vengeful spirits. In this version, the posse caught up with Moses Jr. but had no intention of bringing him back to face charges. Instead, heeding the dog whistle call of Judge Mizell, they planned to see justice served vigilante style. They placed a ploughshare around Moses Jr.'s neck, placed him inside a sack, rowed out into Lake Conway and tossed him overboard. When Moses Jr. managed the surprising feat of freeing himself from both the sack and ploughshare and started swimming back to the shore, the three men opened fire on him, ensuring he would not reach dry land.

Regardless of which version of the story you choose to believe, they both agree on the ending: Moses Jr. met his end in Lake Conway. According to a Barber descendant, Moses Jr.'s body was found near a pond on South Ferncreek Road. For decades, that area was alleged to be haunted by the restless spirit of Moses Jr., who was bound by the waters in which he died. There were even tales of passersby hearing a commotion and seeing someone sink into the waters, only to vanish when rescue attempts were made.

Whatever activity may have once been prevalent at the lake, it seems to have decreased over the last decade or two. Maybe Moses Jr. is finally willing to accept the fact that the feud is over. (It officially ended in the 1940s with a marriage between the two families.) Or maybe it was always just an urban legend, created as a means of keeping children away from a lake at night.

Today, Little Lake Conway (one of the four connected Conway lakes) is popular with those seeking a different sort of thrill—divers intent on exploring the multiple abandoned vehicles, including a school bus, at the bottom of the lake. In a final ironic twist to the tale of Moses Jr., who met his end in those waters at the hands of vigilante lawmen, today, those rusting, submerged vehicles are sometimes used by local police as training for water rescues.

INTERNATIONAL DRIVE

Just over eleven miles in length, the four-lane International Drive (also known as I Drive) begins southwest of downtown Orlando. It's also where you'll find tourists packed bumper to bumper into cars, campers and buses, on their way to and from major attractions, including SeaWorld Orlando, Universal Studios Florida, the Orange County Convention Center, the ICON Orlando Ferris wheel and countless other loudly decorated shops, all vying for vacationers' attention and dollars.

I Drive was originally designed in the 1960s by attorney Finley Hamilton to feed into his Hilton Inn South, which opened in May 1970. At the time, people laughed at what they nicknamed "Finley's Folly," as they failed to see a future in which the area would become one of the most visited tourist destinations on the planet. A year and a half later, in October 1971, when Walt Disney World opened its gates for the first time, it was Hamilton's turn to have a laugh, and laugh he did, long and hard, all the way to the bank.

In 1992, I Drive businesses and local government partnered to create the International Drive Master Transit and Improvement District with a focus on managing growth, transportation and infrastructure development. One of the major projects to emerge from of this alliance was the I Ride bus trolley system.

Today, I Drive is a key artery that endlessly pumps visitors like blood cells through the area. All hours of the day and night, visitors are just dying— some, of course, more literally than others—to check into their hotels and visit the area's museums and attractions.

DOUBLE OCCUPANCY: SUPER 8 BY WYNDHAM

Have you ever wondered what it is about hotels that makes them so prone to ghost stories? Sure, it's one thing to connect hauntings to the once-opulent and historically significant hotels that, in their heydays, hosted the rich and powerful, celebrities, business moguls and political movers and shakers. Those relics of another time, whether they are left to decay or are reborn, might feel to us like they deserve a good ghost story or two. But what about all the other hotels and motels in Orlando (which, at the time of this writing, total more than 480, with over 130,000 rooms)?

Exterior of the Wyndham Super 8 on International Drive. *Photograph by the author.*

Author Colin Dickey offers us the following thoughts on the matter in his book *Ghostlands*: "Stare down a long hotel corridor and you'll feel something like this: there's something uncanny about the very nature of a hotel, its endless, involuntary repetition of home-seeming spaces, rooms that could almost be home but are always somehow slightly off."

Uncanny indeed, and all the more so when one finds that their not-quite home of a hotel room already has another not-quite occupant, which brings us to the long-standing urban legend of room 206 at the Super 8 Motel on International Drive.

Over the years (and under different ownership), room 206 has picked up something of a reputation for itself. Some of the activity reported in the room, including faucets turning on by themselves; the room temperature becoming frigidly cold (even when the air-conditioning is off); feelings of uneasiness, as if being watched, and voices caught on EVP recordings, are all fairly typical of other allegedly haunted hotel rooms. What makes this one unique are the multiple reports from guests of the bed shaking, feeling another person climb into the bed beside them and discovering, even right after the bed has been made, the impression of a body that either was or still is lying there.

Still, for both its similarities and its one significant difference from other instances of haunted hotel rooms, this one seems more appropriately classified as an urban legend. For one thing, an extensive search of old newspapers and other documents failed to produce any death, be it natural or violent, that would connect the specific room in question to a haunting. Coupled with the fact that none of the current or former staff at the hotel interviewed about unusual happenings in room 206 or elsewhere on the property had anything to report, either on or off the record, this case strikes this author as one that should be put to bed.

Of course, visitors are welcome to decide for themselves, just be sure to document any unusual activity. For those with a taste for haunted hospitality, the area boasts plenty of other options, including the Crowne Plaza Hotel, where a full-bodied apparition has been seen in room 621; the former Peabody Hotel (now the Hyatt Regency Orlando); and the Cassadaga Hotel (see page 117). For those willing to travel a bit farther, the Lakeside Inn in Mount Dora is also well worth a visit, not only for its ghosts but also for being the oldest continually operating hotel in the state of Florida.

DREDGING UP THE PAST: *TITANIC:* THE ARTIFACT EXHIBITION

If ghosts, as some believe, are brought forth into the material world by tragic events, it's hard to imagine a peacetime catastrophe better suited to creating those conditions than the sinking of the *Titanic* on April 14, 1912. Per the U.S. committee that investigated the sinking, 1,517 lives were lost, 832 of which were passengers, and the other 685 crew members. More than a century after the ship that was touted as unsinkable came to rest on the ocean floor, few single disasters in modern history can claim to have the same ongoing cultural impact. And in Orlando, where there's a highly romanticized, widely held fascination with the disaster, it was only a matter of time before someone found a way to turn it into a ticketed attraction. G. Michael Harris was that someone, and on April 10, 1999, he opened the first permanent *Titanic* exhibition in Orlando. The timing was not coincidental, as the year prior had seen the release of the Academy Award–winning film *Titanic*. Interest in the maritime tragedy was running at a new high.

After the exhibit was opened and artifacts began to arrive, reports of unusual happenings began to spread. Lights would flicker, and temperatures would fluctuate unexpectedly. (Both can be attributed to electrical issues.) Orbs of light, unseen by the naked eye, showed up regularly in photographs, although such orbs are often discounted as the result of reflections from dust particles and tiny flying insects. As for the distinct and overpowering briny scent that some visitors have reported, is it possible that knowing the fate of the doomed ship and the recovered objects aboard it creates this subconscious olfactory association?

Even if all of the previously mentioned phenomena can be satisfactorily explained away, the appearances of various apparitions of individuals who perished abord the *Titanic*, which have been witnessed on more than one occasion and by more than observer, are a bit harder to dismiss. One of these apparitions is apparently that of the bushy-bearded English newspaper editor and investigative journalism pioneer William Thomas Stead. Is he sending one final dispatch from the other side?

The second and more interactive of the two spirits is that of seven-year-old Catherine Johnson, who may occasionally tug on dresses, pants legs and sleeves; move objects; and bang loud objects together. Perhaps she does this

Within *Titanic*: The Artifact Exhibition, rooms and common areas of the ship have been recreated. Are they still visited by some of those who once sailed aboard the doomed ship? *Photograph by the author.*

in a posthumous attempt to get the attention and assistance that did not arrive in time for her and so many of her fellow passengers. Whatever keeps her bound to this plane of existence, the staff has attempted to make her stay more comfortable by providing her with a Raggedy Ann doll to play with.

When the artifact exhibit reopened in January 2012 at its current location at 7324 International Drive, the paranormal activity continued. Attraction owner Premier Exhibitions realized that rather than being a bane, the hauntings connected to its *Titanic* artifacts could actually present a boon in the form of ghost tours offered throughout the year, especially around the Halloween season. In an official press release from the company, it willingly admitted to the rumors that "for the past five years, staff members at *Titanic: The Experience* have encountered some strange and unanswerable events within the exhibition." The release went on to explain that the organization had partnered with paranormal investigators, who "claimed to have found conclusive evidence of paranormal activity generated by those passengers and crew who sailed on the legendary ship the evening she met her fate."

Those within the organization who have had experiences and encounters there include Kerri Drake, the general manager of *Titanic*: The Experience; Joe Zimmer, an actor and exhibit general manager; Jac LeDoux, the floor manager and director of actors; and several other staff members. Zimmer shared with Spectrum News 13 reporters that he has seen a man wearing an officer's uniform by the first window of the ship's deck section of the exhibit, which is kept between sixty and sixty-five degrees Fahrenheit for effect. He also explained that a heavy metal chain inside the building begins to swing only when the subject of hauntings and the paranormal is discussed.

Does all of this reported activity leave you with the sinking sensation that it's just part of the act, or are you persuaded that the information recounted here represents just the tip of the iceberg, so to speak? Those wishing to weigh the evidence and decide for themselves should check the website for upcoming ghost tours and investigations.

4

WINTER PARK

As with just about every neighborhood and city in and around (and including) Orlando, the city of Winter Park was not born with that name. Originally, it was called Lakeview back in 1858, when David Mizell Jr. purchased an eight-acre parcel of land there. By 1870, it had been renamed Osceola, and in 1881, Loring Chase and Oliver Chapman together bought six hundred acres of land there and began plotting the town they named Winter Park. Four years later, a committee of Congregational ministers seeking to bring an educational institution to the area succeeded in establishing Rollins College, which is the oldest higher education facility in Florida (therefore technically making Winter Park the state's oldest college town). Among the many distinguished graduates of Rollins are Rhodes, Fulbright, Goldwater and Truman Scholars; a Nobel laureate; and one iconic, kind, red cardigan–wearing children's television show host known the world over as Mister Fred Rogers.

The city was chartered in 1887 as a winter resort for wealthy northerners and has continued to draw visitors and vacationers since that time. With beautiful, serene lakes, towering old trees, shopping and dining and cultural offerings, including the Charles Hosmer Morse Museum, the city, true to its original plan, continues to draw visitors and vacationers. Is it any wonder that some of those who visit and relocate there become so attached that they keep going about their daily lives there even long after those lives have ended?

ANNIE RUSSELL, STARRING IN "THE HAUNTING OF ANNIE RUSSELL THEATRE"

Cemeteries and burial grounds, historically significant buildings, hotels and places that are liminal in nature, all of these, as we've explored, help set the stage for hauntings. But there is another type of structure that does so more literally: theaters. For one thing, they are designed for us to witness something take place—rows of seats configured around a stage or screen. And what we witness there occurs at the place where our world of everyday experience intersects with a different world, one conceived, imagined and executed by writers, directors, producers and troupes of actors. If the stage is, by nature, a portal between worlds through which the living pass, could it serve the same purpose for those who are no longer living?

Among the many who would agree that such a thing is plausible are those who've visited and been visited in the Annie Russell Theater at Rollins College (which happens to be the oldest recognized college in the state of Florida).

Annie was born in 1864 (or 1869, as she sometimes preferred) in Dublin, Ireland. Her family moved to Canada, where Annie's father, John, passed away shortly thereafter. At the age of seven, Annie made her stage debut in Montreal in the play *Miss Moulton*. Following her success, her family moved to New York, where she was cast in a juvenile production of *HMS Pinafore*, eventually as the female lead. She went on to tour the West Indies, where she played a variety of roles, and upon returning to New York, she appeared at Madison Square Garden as the leading lady in the play *Esmeralda*, a role she reprised more than nine hundred times. Other roles she enjoyed included Puck from Shakespeare's *A Midsummer Night's Dream* and Viola from the bard's *Twelfth Night*.

While Annie's career continued to ascend, making her one of the best-known and best-paid actresses of her time, she suffered continual setbacks and disappointments in her personal life, including a first marriage to an abusive husband that took a heavy toll on her health and a second equally unhappy marriage to a philanderer.

In 1910, Annie joined the New Theater Company in New York (backed by J. Pierpont Morgan). It was here that she met and became friendly with Mary Louise Curtis (whose father had founded the Curtis Publishing Company), and Mary's fiancé Edward W. Bok (the publisher of the *Ladies Home Journal* who later gifted Central Florida with Bok tower). The Boks encouraged Russell to move to Winter Park in 1929 and recuperate from both a broken hip and a broken marriage (having divorced her second husband after twenty-five years).

Thus, Russell arrived in Florida. In 1931, after seeing a production of *Candide* by the Rollins Players, she and fellow patron of the arts B.J. Thomas decided to approach the president of Rollins College about the need for a top-notch theater in Winter Park. The idea was enthusiastically accepted, and Annie's friend Mary Louise Bok provided $100,000 toward the endeavor. On January 9, 1932, Russell helped place the cornerstone, which contained, among other items, photographs of the actress from her various roles. She also performed there and received a standing ovation on

Photograph of Annie Ellen Russell, circa 1899. *Wikimedia Commons.*

the theater's packed opening night on May 29, 1932. Sadly, Russell had just four years to teach and enjoy productions at the theater named in her honor. On January 16, 1936, she died of pneumonia.

Now, nearly ninety years later, if accounts are to be believed, Annie still isn't quite ready to take her final bow. Much of the reported activity centers on what used to be Annie's private changing room on the second floor of the theater, where there are not infrequent reports of a female apparition. During one the renovations to the theater, that private dressing room, which was accessible only by a stairway, was converted into an electrical closet. (It's no longer accessible following remodeling of the theater in 2011).

Firsthand, unexplained experiences at the theater abound. One woman who worked at the Annie Russell Scene Shop as a student remembers removing a troublesome strip of molding, after which the emergency door slowly swung halfway open. Despite having a self-closing mechanism, the door remained ajar, as if someone was holding it open. The woman and her friend who was with her at the time looked quizzically at each other, trying to figure out what was happening. Finally, the woman called out, asking Annie to shut the door, and as if in response, the door swung shut, leaving both girls in stunned silence.

Yet another story puts Annie in the role of a benevolent, protective spirit, looking out for the well-being of those within her beloved theater. Olivia

Exterior of the Annie Russell Theater. *Photograph by the author.*

Horn shared a story that had been told to her about a strange message that was spray-painted on the stage-right wall back in 1962. Though some of the message was illegible, the phrases "electrocuted" and "broke his back" were still visible. These, Horn says, relate to two men who were working on a set late one night. One of the two was on a ladder, hanging lights, while the other was working elsewhere in the building. The man on the ladder felt a tug on his pants leg and expected it to be his friend, but he saw no one there when he looked down behind him. After once again ascending the ladder, he inadvertently grabbed an electrical wire, the shock of which threw him to the ground. His friend, having heard the commotion, rushed out and called the nearest hospital for an ambulance. It was then that he was told an elderly woman had already requested one a few minutes earlier. This seemed bizarre, since the two male students were certain they'd been there alone. Thankfully, the injured student survived, and some believe he has Annie to thank for that.

Another experience shared by multiple individuals and attributed to Annie's ongoing involvement with the theater that bears her name claims that her favorite seat in the theater (located on the right side of the balcony, third row down and second seat in) is said to fold down and remain that way either the night before or during some productions, supposedly a sign of ghostly approval. At other times, the chair has been heard squeaking and rocking, and late at night, in the darkened theater, one set of hands clapping has been heard issuing from the direction of the seat. The seat folding up and down more than once, the sound of shuffling feet and a strange mist were all supposedly captured on video filmed in 2006 by the group known as the Peace River Ghost Tracker, but following their weekend-long investigation, they discovered that all of their audio and video recordings had been erased.

Rumor has it that the activity around the chair is noticed not just by humans but also by canines. On more than one occasion, when former lighting designer and production manager Jim Fulton brought his golden retriever into the theater, it ran to sit in front of and stare at the empty seat, as if, perhaps, anticipating a Scooby snack for its help in solving a mystery.

Other groups that have conducted investigations of the theater include two teams from White Light Investigations who visited back in 2005. Their experiences, which included encountering orbs of light and cold spots coming from the storage areas under the stage, led them to believe that Annie is still present and active at the theater.

LIFELIKE: THE ALBIN POLASEK MUSEUM AND SCULPTURE GARDENS

If you've visited the home and studio of the world-famous sculptor Albin Polasek, the phrase "hauntingly beautiful" might seem like an apt description of both his artwork and the property where he spent the last portion of his life creating it. Perhaps it's not surprising that several staff members at the museum believe that Polasek's spirit has lingered there since he passed away in 1965. With over two hundred of his sculptures as well as other treasured personal belongings on the premises, he certainly left behind enough of his own blood, sweat and tears to create the kind of connection that transcends death. The most intriguing unexplained happening recorded there, however, doesn't have as much to do the artist's tears as it does with a tear that appeared without explanation on the cheek of Jesus.

The story, as printed in *Park Ave* magazine, says that in 1997, a visitor to the museum took a picture of Polasek's famous Stations of the Cross, a series of circular sculptures that the artist spent three years creating for the St. Celia

Stations of the Cross at the Albin Polasek Museum and Sculpture Garden. *Photograph by the author.*

Cathedral in Omaha, Nebraska. In one of the photographs, Jesus appeared to be crying, a single tear suspended on his cheek. The staff was baffled and could offer no rational explanation as to how the tear appeared there.

Interestingly, this is not the only instance of weeping religious icons in Central Florida. Tarpon Springs, near Tampa, has its own weeping Icon of St. Nicholas that shed tears during the Christmas seasons between 1970 and 1973.

HARRY P. LEU GARDENS

In 1936, Harry and Mary Jane Leu purchased a historic home (originally built in 1858 as a home for the Mizell family), along with forty acres of land.

Harry P. Leu house. *Photograph by the author.*

Mr. Leu's position as the owner of a successful industrial supply company allowed him and his wife to travel the globe, and they brought back from these travels rare and exotic plants and seeds for their gardens. Today, those gardens have blossomed into nothing short of a horticultural treasure, with over two thousand different specimens and species spanning the full alphabet of flora, from aroids to zinnias.

In addition to the house and the gardens, the property also included the Mizell family cemetery (with thirty-six marked and unmarked graves dating to the 1860s), a butterfly garden, the *Citrus Statue* (dedicated to all citrus workers), the curator's office (converted from a servant's residence), the *Doves of Peace* statue near the White Garden, the garden house, the boardwalk and gazebo at Lake Rowena known as the Wyckoff Overlook and the famous fifty-foot floral clock imported from Scotland in 1966 (donated by the Kiwanis Club of Orlando).

When the Leus deeded the house and gardens to the City of Orlando in 1961, some believe that the city came into some rather intangible assets as well in the form of former residents still roaming the property.

Virtually all of the activity reported by both visitors and staff centers on the family home. Along with unusual EMF readings and temperature fluctuations (cold spots) in the upstairs bedrooms, the most commonly cited experience is the sound of phantom footsteps on the second-story porch. Some of the guides have witnessed apparitions in and around the home as well. It is generally assumed that the ghosts on the premises are the spirits of Harry and Mary Jane, who might be checking in to make sure that the city is meeting its obligation by keeping the gardens open to the public.

5

Farther North

Maitland and Longwood

Would it be at all surprising to learn that Maitland, one of the oldest incorporated municipalities in Central Florida, didn't actually originate under that name? Prior to becoming the site of Fort Maitland back in 1838, it was known by its Seminole name, Fumecheliga (meaning "Musk Mellon Place"). Later, the area around the fort became known as Lake Maitland. (Like Sanford farther north, Lake Maitland was named for a man who never actually lived there, Captain William Seton Maitland. He was slain in a battle near Tampa.)

In the fort's early days, the only feasible way to reach it and the rest of Central Florida was via boat from Jacksonville down the St. John's River. Following the Civil War, in 1873, George Packwood received the first property deed in the city and erected a town hall where the city hall stands today. The railroad and hotels brought new residents and visitors to the area (including Presidents Grover Cleveland and Chester Arthur).

As it was in other nearby cities, citrus was the reigning industry in Maitland for a time. In the 1950s, when the Martin Marietta Corporation relocated to the area, it brought its employees and their families, many of whom became residents of Lake Maitland (which officially dropped "Lake" from its name in 1959).

The history of Longwood similarly extends back to Indigenous people, who may have used the ancient cypress known as the Senator as a marker. (The tree, believed to have been one of the oldest on earth, met its end after more than two thousand years in an accidental fire in 2012.) Following the pattern of other towns throughout Central Florida, like Orlando and Sanford, the first settlements near Longwood began around military forts. In the 1850s, between the end of the Seminole Wars and the beginning of the Civil War, those settlers expanded outward to the area that would become Longwood.

The long and short of all this is that wherever there is a long history of conflict, upheaval and change, there's a certainty that if one scratches the surface, they will find a treasure trove of local legends and ghost stories.

SCREAM QUEEN: THE ENZIAN THEATER

While Annie Russell may still be making posthumous cameos at her eponymous theater in Winter Park, she is not the only source of ghostly drama in town. Visitors to the Enzian Theater in Maitland might find themselves witness to a different and more unsettling performance.

First, a bit of background on the theater, which has become a much-loved local institution. Founded in 1985 by the Tiedtke family, it started life as a repertory house, showing up to a dozen classic films each week along with the occasional live show. In 1989, management decided to take a risk on showing first-run independent films as more of an art house venue. The gamble paid off, and the innovative small theater was put in the national spotlight as the only nonprofit, alternative movie theater in Central Florida. A few years later, it became home to the Oscar-qualifying Florida Film Festival. Even on less star-studded nights, the theater provides engaging and creative programming throughout the year, and visitors can always see the other kinds of stars from the Eden Bar connected to the theater, which offers alfresco dining and drinks. Not surprisingly, the theater is loved by locals, film buffs and anyone looking for an ideal spot to hang out with friends or have a date.

But someone, it seems, has been hanging around long after their final curtain. Her appearance is said to be both infrequent and contingent on multiple factors. Some say that she appears only on moonless nights. Others say she visits the theater only on the opening night of new films. And still others claim that both of those conditions must be met before the ghost known as the screaming head of the Enzian Theater will take center stage.

All who have seen her suggest that the best time to look for her is approximately 1:00 a.m., when her dismembered head shows up in the

Exterior of the Enzian Theater. *Photograph by the author.*

north corner of the theater and then floats around to the other corners while screaming. It eventually disappears through the wall and into what was previously the kitchen of Nicole St. Pierre (today, the Eden Bar).

There is no consensus about who the head belongs to or why she haunts the theater, though some have speculated that she is attached to either the theater or some other building that may have once occupied the same space. Whatever her motive, in death, she is clearly not concerned about observing good movie theater etiquette, which suggests that one not add their own bloodcurdling soundtrack.

Shawn, one of the managers at the theater, has not had the displeasure of encountering the screaming head himself, nor has he had any other paranormal or unexplained experiences at the theater, but he confirmed that many of those currently employed at the Enzien firmly believe the location to be haunted.

DEATH IMITATING LIFE IMITATING ART: MAITLAND ART CENTER

Considered by many a visionary artist and architect, André Smith is known today as much for his work as for having established an art colony in 1937 along Lake Sybelia. Originally called the Research Studio, the facility has evolved over time into what is now known as the Art Center at Art and History Museums Maitland (A&H). Set within the distinctive Mayan Revival–style compound are galleries, an event space and rural telephone museum and the art center, which has stayed true to its founder's vision of providing studio space for working artists. More than a few there believe Smith still stops by from time to time to make sure the center's operations are living up to his standards—a nifty trick given than Smith passed away while he was on the campus in 1959.

Smith's apparition has been noticed numerous times by visitors and staff who have seen him standing or wandering throughout the grounds and studios. Others, including several of the artists in residence, have claimed they felt Smith's presence, and some have even smelled the smoke from one of his cigars.

James Cook, a potter at the art center during the 1980s, even claimed he received a posthumous critique of his work. Hearing the voice of Smith discussing Cook's work with a woman, the potter was inspired to try something new with hist artwork, which resulted in a successful new approach for him.

Another artist, Bruce Orr, also said he had an encounter with Smith. While preparing to leave his studio one night, he heard the sound of glass shattering and spun around in time to see (and see through) a transparent apparition of the center's founding father. Shaken, Orr made a quick exit and locked

This page: A&H Maitland is distinctive for its Mayan Revival–style architecture—and for its ghosts. *Photographs by the author*.

the door behind him. There's no word yet on what impact, if any, the experience had on his creative output.

Even the art center's former CEO and executive director Andrea Bailey Cox had her own encounter with Smith's ghost. In an interview with Alejandro Rojas for a *Huffpost* article, she recounted arriving at the campus early one morning and seeing a man through a window in one of the casements. As she came around the other side of the building, expecting someone to be there, she found instead that the stranger had vanished. Rather than being disturbed by it, she considered Smith's presence there as a sign that he is happy with the way his legacy is being preserved.

STILL WATERS RUN DEEP: WATERHOUSE RESIDENCE MUSEUM

As it turns out, the art center is not the only building under the aegis of A&H Maitland with a haunted history. Just down the road from the main museums, next to Lake Lily, is what some ghost hunters and paranormal enthusiasts have called one of the most active haunted house in Central Florida.

Of course, it didn't start out that way. Back in 1884, carpenter William Waterhouse built the two-and-a-half-story, L-shaped structure as a home for his family, which included his wife, Sarah, and their two children. Charles and Stella continued to live in the house after their parents' death. Additions to the house were made in 1908, 1910, 1930 and once more in the 1950s.

Stella continued to reside there into her nineties. In the 1980s, the home was donated to the City of Maitland, and in 1983, it was listed in the National Register of Historic Places. The home is considered the oldest in Maitland and also one of the city's few remaining examples of nineteenth-century vernacular architecture. Since coming under the management of A&H Maitland, the home has been reopened as the Waterhouse Residence Museum and painstakingly restored to provide visitors with an inside look at Victorian-era middle-class living.

The Waterhouse Residence Museum. *Photograph by the author.*

The Waterhouse Museum has come to be regarded as another one of Maitland's cultural gems, but arguably, the greatest testament to A&H Maitland's accuracy in showcasing daily life during the Gilded Age comes not from Yelp and other online reviews but rather from the home's former residents, who seem content to continue going about their own daily lives there.

There is, of course, the general tell-tale signs of their presence in the strange noises, cold spots and flickering lights that both visitors and staff have experienced in the home. More specific to the Waterhouse residence are the frequent reports of an old woman looking out from her second-floor window over Lake Lily. According to exhibitions manager Katie Benson, this is believed to be the spirit of Stella, who enjoyed that particular view for the better part of a century.

Inside the home, in Stella's bedroom, more than a few guests have encountered a different spectral figure, that of a man dressed in gray, moving across the room. Some staff members also claim to have witnessed the bed in this room moving on its own, and others who have opened the museum in the morning have discovered that the bed mysteriously changed its location over the course of the day.

THE CAPTAIN AND HIS CAT: THE INSIDE-OUTSIDE HOUSE

If you recall the Rogers building from earlier in this book (page 30), you might also remember that architecturally unusual buildings seem more prone to not only draw puzzled looks from neighbors and those passing by but also become the source of urban legends and ghost stories. Once again, that may be the case with what's become known as the Inside-Outside House, now located at 141 West Church Avenue in Longwood.

The house's moniker comes from its oddly inverse design. Its structural framing is exposed on the exterior of the house, somewhat like an exoskeleton, its panels bolted together in the style known as shiplap (wood paneling with a groove cut into the top and bottom of each board so that they overlap to create a waterproof seal). The interior of the house is more like what one would expect on the outside, with stucco over tongue-and-groove siding. Decorative finishes along the front porch, balcony and roofline make the house still harder to miss.

One of the earliest known examples of a prefabricated house in the United States, the structure was originally built in Massachusetts and then shipped to Florida, where it was reassembled in Altamonte Springs as the home of retired sea captain W. Pierce. Pierce and his wife, along with their beloved black cat Brutus, lived at the top of the wooden spiral staircase on the home's second floor, while the first floor was used as a cabinet shop. After Pierce's death, another family occupied the home for a time, but after that, it was left vacant and fell into disrepair.

When the Longwood Historical Society rescued the building from demolition in 1973 and relocated it to its present address, it arrived with not only its distinctive architectural design but also, if local lore is to be believed, the spirits of its former residents. Intense cold spots (even when the air-conditioning is turned off), voices without any discernable source and footsteps have all been reported and are interpreted by some as evidence that the captain still occupies the building. His black cat Brutus has been spotted from time to time in one of the upper windows and has been felt brushing up against the legs of women wearing dresses. One visitor to the shop remembered seeing a rocking chair on the second floor spring backward as if something cat-sized had just leapt from it.

After restoration, the building housed an antique shop. Then in the early 1980s, it became the Culinary Cottage. Pamela Redditt worked there from 1991 until she and her husband, Tom, purchased the business in 1995. Later on, they changed the name to the Cottage Gift Shop, which operates there currently.

Pamela had heard tales of the old home being haunted but didn't give such stories much credence until she had a series of her own experiences there. The first of these, she said, occurred when a Romanian crystal bowl she had ordered was set on the mantel as she locked up for the day. The following morning, she found it underneath a glass-top table, remarkably unbroken. Both the location of the item and the lack of any damage was enough to give her pause. Something similar happened again, involving a collectible replica of the Inside-Outside House. Pamela found it at the foot of the narrow, wooden spiral staircase (also called a captain's stairway) to the second floor, which she mentioned seems to be a focal point for the ghostly activity within the building. "It seemed," she mused, "as if the captain wanted to inspect and make sure he approved of the replica of his home." Author Joyce Elson Moore recorded additional experiences that Pamela has had at her store. The first of these occurred about a year after Pamela started working in the house. One day, while she was on the second floor, she felt a deep chill

This page: Exterior of the Inside-Outside House and the captain's stairway, which has been a focal point of ghostly activity within the building. *Photographs by the author*.

behind her (even though the room did not have air-conditioning), and she sensed someone or something wordlessly conveying to her that her presence there was unwelcome. She announced that she was leaving the room and did so with haste. Months later, a customer told Pamela about experiencing a similar sensation on the first floor.

Pam's next run-in with the unexplained at the Inside-Outside House came the following summer, when she was picking up some merchandise from a tray that had slipped out of her hands. As she bent down, she heard a deep voice give a drawn-out "yes" from directly behind her. Startled, she searched for the source of the voice but failed to find anyone inside. The windows were shut, which made it virtually impossible that she could have heard the voice at all, let alone so clearly, from outside.

On another occasion, one winter evening after she had turned off one of the lamps, Pamela saw the silhouette of a figure standing by a table near the front door. As she had done previously in the upstairs room, she said out loud that she was leaving and quickly did just that.

Pamela shared one final experience she had while working upstairs at the house alone. It was evening at the time, and she heard a door open and close loudly. Thinking it was her husband, Tom, she called down to him. She decided to call him at home. When he answered, she knew he couldn't have entered the Inside-Outside House. She waited upstairs until her husband arrived at the shop to escort her home.

Tom, who has worked at the store with his wife from time to time, remains skeptical of the presence of Captain Pierce, Brutus or any other spirits at the house. He has not personally experienced anything that he would consider outré or supernatural. Still, he notes, this doesn't keep the couple from getting calls from time to time from paranormal investigators and authors writing books about haunted places, like this one.

STAYING POWER: THE LONGWOOD VILLAGE INN

If you're establishing a new town and want to draw affluent visitors and potential residents, you need an impressive place for them to stay. Longwood founder Edward Warren Henck no doubt knew this when he commissioned Josiah B. Clouster to construct the town's first hotel in 1883. The large, three-story, framed vernacular-style building with Italianate influences was put on the market in 1885 as construction neared completion. It was purchased by Carlos Cushing, who lived nearby in what is today Altamonte Springs, and by 1886, the building was finished and welcoming its first guests as the Waltham. The hotel proudly featured amenities such as electric bells, bathrooms and upscale furnishings, all conveniently located at the junction of two railroads.

The hotel was a success and entertained visitors during the winter season. Unfortunately, like the area as a whole, it fell on hard times and closed following the two freezes that occurred on December 26, 1894, and February 7, 1895 (known together as the Great Freeze). Charles W. Entzminger acquired, refurbished and reopened the hotel in 1910 and sold it to Bass Shoe Company salesman George Clark twelve years later.

Clark is credited with revitalizing the hotel and infusing it with his infectious enthusiasm. Sadly, when he was conspicuously absent from an ice cream social he had organized there on April 3, 1923, to celebrate the close of the tourist season, his wife went looking for him and discovered that he had suffered a bad fall toward the back of the building. He died as a result of his injuries the next day.

Following Clark's death, the hotel has undergone significant changes (including ownership) more than half a dozen times. In 1923, Fred Clark took over the establishment, which he renamed the Orange and Black. During this time, the hotel earned a reputation for hosting gambling, whiskey and sex workers. Ed Crocker became the next owner in 1926 as part of a syndicate (of which Baseball Hall of Famer Joe Tinker was a member) and renamed it the Longwood Hotel. In the 1930s, Florence Bunker Clark, George's widow, regained the title to the property. In 1947, Clark sold the property to F.S. Saunders, who, in turn, sold it to restaurateur Maximillian Shepard. After the building's run as a popular restaurant, George Barr stepped up to the plate in 1952 and took a swing at owning the building, which he converted into a school for baseball umpires. By 1957, the hotel was back on the auction block, where it was sold to Louis T. Hunt. He and his wife, Bobbie Jo (who had their wedding ceremony there), managed the restaurant and lived on the second floor. When Bobbi Jo passed on, she left the business to her son, who ran the hotel as a low-income boardinghouse primarily for migrants. Shortly thereafter, in 1964, the hotel and other spots within Longwood became locations where the film *Johnny Tiger* was shot.

In 1972, Mrs. Robert S. Bradford bought the hotel. A founding member of the Longwood Historic Society, Bradford changed the hotel's name to the Longwood Village Inn and succeeded in having it dedicated on July 26, 1976, as a Florida Historical Landmark (and also added, in 1984, to the

Exterior of the Longwood Village Inn. *Photograph by the author.*

U.S. National Register of Historic Places). After the hotel, which became a popular venue for weddings and other events, was restored and reopened, it was sold once more to Mr. and Mrs. George St. Laurent Sr. from New Jersey. The couple managed the hotel until Mr. St. Laurent Sr.'s death, after which it was donated to Cornell University in 1978. Since then, the building has housed offices under the management of Homevest Realty.

To summarize, in this sometimes-hotel (which is both historically and architecturally unique), the greatest joys (such as weddings and other celebrations), along with the most bitter tragedies (untimely deaths), have all played out. Is it really any wonder that it became a prime candidate for a haunting?

Author Dave Lapham dug deeper into the haunted history of the Longwood Village Inn in his book *Ghosthunting Florida*. During their research, Lapham and his sensitive companion, Joanne, made the hotel one of the many stops on their "tour de forces from beyond." In the company of Ann, an agent liaison for Lenny Layland of Homevest Realty, who was well-versed in the property's history, Joanne first wandered through the building, identifying a few different areas where she picked up on otherworldly vibes. She then compared her notes with Ann's.

The first spot to register on Joanne's supernatural radar was the women's bathroom past the reception area, where she saw a tall, thin, gray-haired man in a dark suit. She continued to experience a presence (or presences) on the stairway and stopped on the second floor after detecting something connected to the roof. On the third floor, she received intense feelings from rooms 308, 309 and 310. In room 309, she specifically sensed a male presence that was not at all pleased with having his personal space invaded. Back on the first floor, she sat down in a chair in the conference room and sensed part of the same spirit she had noticed earlier by the ladies' room.

Ann then confirmed and connected Joanne's experiences with prior happenings. The smartly dressed man on the first floor, she said, was believed to be the spirit of none other than the hotel's previous owner George Clark. Ann shared that other psychics had similarly mentioned feeling energy on the stairway. As for the roof, three men had recently been driving by the hotel at approximately 10:00 p.m., when they noticed what appeared to be a man in a three-piece suit standing there. They were concerned enough that they pulled over, called up to him not to jump and eventually called the

Lobby of the Longwood Village Inn. *Photograph by the author.*

police. Of course, by the time the officer arrived, the figure on the roof had vanished. Apparently, this sort of thing happened frequently enough that the officer shrugged it off and said it was probably a ghost.

To these various stories, Ann added some of her own, which included an experience she had while staying overnight in the building with friends to capture orbs. They were startled when they all clearly heard a disembodied male voice tell them, "You gotta believe!" Another evening, while she was doing work on the third floor as a storm raged outside, Ann heard what sounded like an invisible tea cart rolling down the hallway past the room she was in. Lastly, she and two other women witnessed a strange light take shape toward the top of the northern wall of the lobby. They watched as it took the shape of a child's face and then leapt off the wall into the center of the room and disappeared, which sent the women running and screaming.

The building has been investigated by professional teams, including the Southern Paranormal Research Society (SPRS) for the Travel Channel show *Shadow Hunting*. SPRS and others who have investigated the space believe that one or more guests continue to lodge there, decades past their checkout time.

APOPKA

THE MCBRIDE AND GROOM: LONGWOOD MANOR

When you think about it, it seems inevitable than an old ballroom-style, Queen Anne Victorian home, surrounded by ancient oaks, originally located across from the oldest cemetery in Apopka, would become a source of both curiosity and ghost stories. That certainly is the case with the McBride house (now an event venue known as Longwood Manor).

The four-thousand-square-foot home, originally built in 1903 for the Eldrige family, was bought in the 1920s by Dr. Thomas McBride and his wife, Helen. In addition to serving as the couple's family residence, the home also provided a location for Dr. McBride's medical practice, where, as one of Apopka's first physicians, he served the needs of the community for five decades, delivering, by his own estimate, over one thousand babies.

Helen McBride was an accomplished pilot who flew competitively, and during World War II, she trained other future pilots, including some who went on to fly planes into combat. In 1956, Helen was involved in a deadly conflict of her own when an argument with an airline ticket agent spun out of control. The ticket agent with National Airlines in Orlando, identified as Charles Richard Green, is said to have slapped Helen during the heated dispute, and she, in return, shot him dead there in the family home.

An article from the *Orlando Evening Star*, dated Saturday, May 26, 1956, reveals a more complex relationship between the two parties. Green, according to the article, was her partner in her aviation training business. A circuit court grand jury indicted Mrs. McBride on a first-degree murder charge, even though she claimed she acted in self-defense. Later, after a four-day trial, she was acquitted.

Following the incident, Helen spent the rest of her life more or less confined to the home, where she passed away in 1961. Dr. McBride continued to practice medicine until he, too, passed away at home in 1978.

For the next several years, the home stood vacant, accumulating dust and stories. Slated for demolition, it was relocated in 1985 to its current location overlooking North Orange Blossom Trail and State Road 436. The following decade, it was updated and renovated to become a restaurant (first the Captain and Cowboy and then Townsend's Plantation). No sooner had it opened its doors than employees and patrons began to notice strange happenings. Intense cold spots and lights going on and off seemingly of their own accord could be attributed to faulty wiring and drafts through an old home. Other occurrences, however, like the sightings of a female apparition in a blue dress descending the stairs and making her way through crowds of diners, are a bit harder to explain.

A former employee of the restaurant recalled one Halloween during which a séance was held on the third floor. The chandeliers swayed violently, casting wild shadows across the ceiling and room, and he described the air as feeling heavy and dense. Unfortunately, while spirits seemed able to materialize at the restaurant, revenue did not. The business went into bankruptcy, from which it did not reemerge, and the building passed another decade without any living inhabitants.

That's not to say that strange activity wasn't noticed there. Unexplained lights and shadowy forms in the windows, alarms tripping from time to time without any evidence of intrusion and even eerie wails and screams—all of these and other curious occurrences made the home once again a source of tales about ghosts and restless spirits. This also made it the ideal place to stage Halloween (faux) haunted houses. Keith Lock of Magical Art and Design was preparing for one such event when he and his team noticed a portrait of the doctor on the wall of what was once the master bedroom on

Inside Longwood Manor, by the stairs leading up to the second and third floors. *Photograph by the author.*

the second floor. Shortly after leaving the room, they heard a loud crash and returned to find the portrait lying face down on the floor, even though no one else had been in the room. Was that a coincidence, or was the doctor trying to draw their attention to an actual haunting?

Similarly, during a Halloween radio broadcast in 1999, the haunting went off script when reporters were subjected to sudden blasts of chilling cold, loud thuds and noises coming from behind a locked door on the third floor.

Perhaps the most unexpected and unexplainable phenomenon is that none of the haunted happenings at what is now known as Longwood Manor have in any way diminished its popularity as a venue for weddings and other events. If, every once in a while, the chandeliers begin to swing wildly without cause during a photo shoot, doors open and close at random and, from time to time, full-bodied apparitions crash the party, no one gets all that upset about it. Rather, folks mostly shrug it off and accept it as part of the charm of hosting events at a haunted location. The consensus seems to be that having to reschedule or losing one's deposit on such a sought-after historic venue is by far more terrifying than ghosts.

6

WALT DISNEY WORLD AND OTHER THEME PARKS

Today, the sprawling entertainment complex of theme parks, hotels and other attractions known collectively as Walt Disney World draws tens of millions of visitors from around the world each year. This unquestionably makes it the best-known and most-visited part of Orlando—so much so that it's virtually impossible to imagine the park existing anywhere else. Back in 1959, however, when Walt began scouting out locations for a second park to follow the model of his Disneyland in Anaheim, California, Orlando was just one of several potential options, and most doubted it was a frontrunner. That allegedly changed when Walt took a flight over the area in November 1963 and saw that the land was situated near the intersection of I-4 and the Florida Turnpike. (Today, those two major arteries meet between the Kirkman Road and Conroy Road exits by the Mall at Millenia.) This, Walt realized, would make his future kingdom highly accessible. So, "X" marked the spot, and he quietly began buying up land under dozens of different names and companies so as not to reveal his plans (which would have caused the price of the land he was acquiring to skyrocket). If that sounds a little bit shady, well, yes—it's hard to argue otherwise. But then, is there really anything more quintessentially Floridian than sketchy real estate deals involving former swampland?

Initially, some news outlets floated the possibility that NASA was behind the buying spree, but it was the *Orlando Sentinel*'s Emily Bavar who got the scoop and broke the story on October 21, 1965. Walt passed away in 1966 from lung cancer before the opening of either Disney World or his

Above: Walt Disney unveiling the plans for his Experimental Prototype Community of Tomorrow (EPCOT). *Courtesy of the Orange County Regional History Center.*

Left: Cinderella Castle inside the Magic Kingdom at Walt Disney World. *Photograph by the author.*

Experimental Prototype Community of Tomorrow (EPCOT). Completing those projects fell to his brother Roy.

Walt Disney World welcomed its first visitors on October 1, 1971, and exactly eleven years later, to the day, EPCOT opened its doors. All of Central Florida, and especially Orlando, was forever changed. In fact, the city has yet to cease being impacted and altered by the parks. Celebration was founded in mid-1990s essentially as its own Disney company town (not entirely unlike the attempted utopian communities like Chicago's Pullman District; Hershey, Pennsylvania; Scotia, California; and others).

The relationship between Walt Disney World, Celebration, Orlando and the state of Florida is in a constant state of flux, but as of this writing (despite the recent dissolution of the Reedy Creek Improvement District in 2023), that Gordian knot has yet to be fully untangled.

Now, ask yourself: Would it further complicate matters if some of the locations connected by this geographic web just happened to be haunted?

HAUNTED MOUSE HOUSE: WALT DISNEY WORLD

Sure, you probably know Disney World as "the most magical place on Earth," and taking the family there is arguably the closest thing we have in modern American culture to making a pilgrimage, but there have been enough reports of strange happenings at various spots throughout the parks to warrant their own special section of this book. Rest assured, though, you won't need the help of a genie or any special app or pass to access these tales—just keep reading.

GEORGE: THE GHOST OF THE CARIBBEAN

One might logically assume that of all the rides at Disney World, the Haunted Mansion would be something like a beacon for spirits at the park. It turns out, however, that it's a pirate's afterlife for the most well-known of Disney's ghosts. Like most ghost stories verging on urban legends, this tale has multiple versions and variations, but they all focus on an unfortunate construction contractor named George who was hired to help build the Pirates of the Caribbean attraction. During construction, George is said to have either fallen from a ladder or been hit by a beam. In either case, the result was the same—George was killed instantly. Given that the ride made its debut at the Magic Kingdom in December 1973, we can assume that this took place earlier that same year.

Most versions of the story connect this mishap to the tower in the "burning city" portion of the ride. According to some sources, cast members actually refer to it as George's Tower and claim that his initials were carved into the base and reappear in spite of all attempts to remove them or cover them with a fresh coat of paint.

In some versions of the story, George's Tower plays another role as something of a ghost indicator. If the light in the tower is switched on in the scene, that apparently means George is going to cause mischief. Alternately, if the door is open behind the animatronic dog with the prison keys in its mouth, that signals forthcoming paranormal activity.

Some say that these animatronic pirates are not the only ones trapped inside the ride. *Photograph by the author.*

What is it that George wants? Apparently—and here, again, all the stories converge—he wants respect, hence the tradition of cast members wishing George a good morning at the start of each day and bidding him farewell before they depart each night. What happens if George doesn't receive his daily affirmations from the living? Most often, he manifests his ire by causing electronic malfunctions and mechanical issues. It's tempting to classify this as harmless mischief—until you consider what happens when hundreds of people who've been standing in line for an hour or more suddenly learn that their wait times have doubled or tripled.

Other antics sometimes attributed to George include sudden chills and whispers coming from empty seats on board the ride. Some hold George responsible for strange ghostly images appearing on monitors and for making prank calls from the ride. Occasionally, he is said to get a bit inappropriate with women riders, who have complained of feeling a tug on their bra straps or receiving a pat on their bottoms.

When things go wrong, it's sometimes nice to have a ghostly fall guy to pin the blame on, but it seems unlikely that every mishap, major or minor, could be George's doing.

According to Nathaniel Eker in an article on the popular *Inside the Magic* blog, since 2005, there has been a noticeable decline in George-related incidents and sightings, which suggests that either the engineers have finally resolved long-standing technical problems or that some thirty years after his undocumented demise, George has had his fill of troublemaking.

A DISNEY DUSTUP

Before exploring any of the other ghosts and urban legends connected to Walt Disney World, it's worth mentioning a particularly disturbing rumor that was confirmed by the *Wall Street Journal* back in October 2018. The story states: "Human ashes have been spread in flower beds, on bushes and on Magic Kingdom lawns; outside the park gates and during fireworks displays; on Pirates of the Caribbean and in the moat underneath the flying elephants of the Dumbo ride."

It's understandable, of course, that someone would want to honor the final wishes of a loved one, friend or family member, even if those wishes involve spreading their ashes at their favorite ride at Walt Disney World. For years, it had been whispered that cremated human remains were sometimes snuck into the park and scattered. But unlike most urban legends, this one turns out to be true, and it happens often enough that there is both a specific code (HEPA Cleanup) and a custom-designed vacuum to address such incidents.

Presumably, it still happens, despite increased security and monitoring

Exterior of the Haunted Mansion inside Walt Disney World. *Photograph by the author.*

on and around rides. As far as which ride is most often the target of this activity, well, in case you couldn't already guess: "Most frequently of all, according to custodians and park workers, they've been dispersed throughout the Haunted Mansion, the 49-year-old attraction featuring an eerie old estate full of imaginary ghosts."

Are these ashes responsible for or directly connected to any of the hauntings inside any of the parks? Surely, it's hard to imagine a better basis for supernatural activity than swirling clouds of dust mingled with human cremains.

WE HAVE ALWAYS LIVED IN THE MANSION

George might get the most attention (lest he cause mayhem at the Pirates ride), but he is not the only one rumored to be haunting the park. There are at least

This photograph made the rounds on the internet, purporting to be an image of a ghost child riding a doombuggy. *Public domain.*

five others that, appropriately enough, reside among the other "999 happy haunts" at the Haunted Mansion.

One of these is known as "the man with the cane." He walks with a noticeable limp and seems not to notice when approached or addressed by guests or cast members. Rather than make any response, he simply dematerializes, leaving witnesses to ponder who this long-distance visitor is and what he's doing at the park. An article on the website Spookeats.com puts forth the idea that he may be the spirit of a World War II pilot who perished while training, when his plane crashed into what today is Bay Lake.

Another spirit that is sometimes spotted in the Mansion is that of a young boy happily riding his own "doombuggy." Like the man with the cane, he disappears when spotted. The boy has been captured in at least one photograph, peeking over the side of his doombuggy at the camera, and he does indeed appear to be smiling and enjoying the ride for all of eternity. This stands in contrast to the spirit of a young boy who is spotted and heard near the exit of the Disneyland (California) version of the Haunted Mansion. That spirit is said to be crying out for his mother who surreptitiously spread his ashes on the ride.

In the first volume of his collection of legends and folklore about the Sunshine State's ghosts, Greg Jenkins adds a few more names to the Mansion's guest list. One is called "the Tuxedo Ghost," who likes to sneak up behind cast members. It is unclear who this particular ghost was in life (possibly a friend or colleague of Walt Disney). Who he was, however, probably matters less to the college student and part-time cast member who was said to have been scared out of her job when she saw the shadow of a man behind her, caught the face of a man in one of the mirrors (though there was no one behind her) and finally felt an ice-cold hand on her shoulder. Jenkins tells of another soul at the Mansion who fell to his death from the ride on one of Walt Disney World's "grad nights" for local high school seniors.

Other tales of actual hauntings among the animatronics at the Mansion include ghosts appearing in the various mirrors throughout the ride (including

One of the animatronic ghosts inside the Haunted Mansion. *Photograph by the author.*

the one at the end, in which the hitchhiking ghosts are projected alongside riders), cast members hearing footsteps while alone after the ride has closed and individuals feeling watched and being touched by an invisible hand.

A WORLD OF FEARS

For sheer creepiness, it's pretty hard to top haunted, possessed and/or cursed dolls (Florida's most famous of which is undoubtedly "Robert the Doll" in Key West). Walt Disney World apparently has not one but two different and very disconcerting stories regarding animated dolls.

Meet Isabella, the doll that some visitors have seen in various windows throughout Liberty Square and also next to door no. 24 inside the Hall of Presidents. The legend, as told by author Kara Michaels, is that the doll was a favorite possession of a young girl who died at the park. Since that time, the doll has been said to shift from location to location and even move on its own.

One inexplicably moving doll inside the park would probably be more than enough to fuel most visitors' nightmares, but it turns out that there may be more than one. According to an article on the website Disney Dining, author Ridley Pearson was given a behind-the-scenes tour of the It's a Small World ride without the lights, music and power. Despite the ride being deactivated, Pearson claims he witnessed two of the dolls moving on their own. A similar account was recalled by Kelly Wilton, who said she was on the ride as a ten-year-old when it malfunctioned. Her boat stopped on its track, and the music slowed down and then sped up while the volume changed, and despite the animatronics having stopped functioning, she distinctly remembers seeing one of the dolls look directly at her and wave one of its hands back and forth. Apparently, even some of the cast members have had similar experiences on the ride. Suffice it to say, it turns out that the most terrifying aspect of the ride might not be trying to get that endlessly looped, eerily cheerful earwig of a song out of one's head.

UNAMUSED: OTHER HAUNTED ATTRACTIONS

For the paranormal enthusiast, there's one more stop worth making within the Magic Kingdom: Tom Sawyer Island. There have been reports that some parts of the island feel slightly disconcerting in ways that visitors find hard to articulate. If that sounds too vague, you can always opt to look for the shadow figures that are alleged to dwell in the caves there, unfettered by any connection to material objects.

Let's go park hopping—next stop, Disney's Hollywood Studios, where we'll be keeping an eye out for the ghost of a former cast member dressed as a bellhop at the Tower of Terror. This spirit has been spotted in the lobby, the loading area and on the ride itself. Accounts vary, but the spirit may appear to be walking in the wrong direction and disappear when approached.

Next on our agenda is Walt Disney's own beloved pet project EPCOT. For haunt hunting, you'll want to orbit the Spaceship Earth ride, where the ghost of a boy and a blond girl are said to play outside the entrance before vanishing. Other sources have said that the two perform their disappearing act on the ride itself.

OK, have you had your fill of Walt Disney World? There's one more park to explore, and the ghost that some claim makes a cameo there is about as big a name as you could imagine. Of course, Universal Studios Florida is no

Every Halloween season, Universal Studios Orlando gets a creepy makeover for Halloween Horror Nights. *Photograph by the author.*

stranger to high-profile stars and celebrities. Does it feel a bit like this author is drawing this one out and savoring the reader's suspense? If so, consider it an homage to the spirit of the master of suspense himself, Alfred Hitchcock.

Though Hitchcock passed away in 1980, ten years later, when Universal Studios Florida opened, it did so with Alfred Hitchcock: The Art of Making Movies as one of its features. It closed, however, without warning on January 3, 2003, and was replaced with Shrek 4D. Since then, more than one person has seen Hitchcock there in the first theater, where the lights turn off and doors shut on their own. Multiple employees at the park have confirmed the filmmaker's presence on the soundstage and elsewhere, the reason being that "he is not happy the ogre replaced his beloved attraction."

7

BEYOND ORLANDO

I f there is one refrain this author heard most from sources and contributors while researching stories for *Haunted Orlando*, it must be, "Oh, you've got to include this one, too, even though it's not technically in Orlando." Often, the suggested sites were not only outside of Orlando but outside of Orange County. All the same, the Oviedo ghost lights, the haunting of launch complex 34 at the Kennedy Space Center and the Spiritualist community of Cassadaga would have been conspicuous for their absence in any book about Orlando-area hauntings. Far more locations, however, did not make it into this book. A short and partial list of those places that didn't make the cut includes the Last Resort biker bar in Daytona, which was frequented by serial killer Aileen Wuornos (and also where she was taken into police custody); the bullet-riddled house in Ocklawaha where Ma Barker and one of her sons met their end after the longest gun battle in FBI history; and the legend of the Devil's Chair in the cemetery near Cassadaga, which has been sufficiently debunked by Mark Muncy in his book *Eerie Florida* (although he is also the first to remind readers that just because that particular story is not credible, that does not mean the cemetery isn't legitimately haunted).

What remains and what follows are a selection of sites from Sanford, Oviedo, Kissimmee and elsewhere that are either significant enough or close enough to Orlando to warrant inclusion.

PARTY OF FIVE:
WOP'S HOPS BREWING COMPANY (SANFORD)

What does a business owner do when they discover that their workplace is deemed haunted? For some, like the owners of Amura, it's an absolute deal breaker. Meanwhile, Hamburger Mary's has extended the idea of inclusivity to encompass the undead, and the Halloween-themed bar Cocktails and Screams has embraced the idea of occasional hauntings in its space (next to the old Carry Hand Funeral Home) as the most on-brand marketing imaginable.

The folks at Wop's Hops have taken yet another approach to dealing with the hauntings on their premises, which is to more or less shrug and go on about business as usual, brewing and serving award-winning beers. Still, with psychics and ghost hunters convinced of at least five different ghosts on the premises, that can be a lot to try to ignore. The building certainly has enough history to account for all of the specters suspected of lingering there. It began life in 1916 as a meat business, after which it was converted into a women's clothing store, a restaurant and, eventually, in the 1940s, Stokes Fish Market, which operated there until 2005. More recently, in 2014, the space became home to Sanford's first microbrewery, which operates there currently.

Within the brewery, various spirits have staked out their own territory. The ghost known as Stephen tends to hang out by the back area of the brewery, specifically in the bathroom and the hallway leading to it. While the brewery itself is dog-friendly, it seems that Stephen might be less so—canines and children reportedly tend to avoid the areas Stephen haunts.

Claudia, who is believed to have worked at the fish market, now spends her afterlife roaming between the brewery and tasting room, along with Jennifer, a sex worker who was allegedly stabbed and strangled to death.

The spirit named David is most often encountered in the beer garden. There is no consensus between psychics about why he was beaten to death (one believes it was for selling tainted horse meat while another believes it was because of his homosexuality). Whatever the reason, both sensitives agree that the result of David's beating was death due to blunt-force trauma.

The fifth and final ghost believed to inhabit the brewery has been more reluctant to make itself known, which has led to speculation that it may be the ghost of a child.

For whatever reason, these and perhaps other visitors from the great beyond seem to enjoy congregating at Wop's Hops every bit as much as the locals do, and neither the living nor the dead seem in any way deterred by the other.

This page: Exterior and interior of Wop's Hops Brewing Company in Sanford. *Photographs by the author.*

A TWO HORSE TOWN (SANFORD)

GHOST HORSE OF CELERY AVENUE

The first of Sanford's two equine spirits is known as the ghost horse of Celery Avenue. The translucent horse is said to appear near Beardall Avenue, galloping down the street, between and through vehicles, only to vanish in front of spectators. Sometimes, the horse is seen on its own, while in other cases, it carries a Native rider. Whether fact or fabrication, this particular haunting might owe its origin to something of a historical mash-up.

The story begins with Sligh Earnest, a blacksmith who owned a massive snow-white draft horse, alleged to weigh upward of 3,200 pounds. When the horse expired, a tractor was needed to haul the animal's body to its final resting place on Celery Avenue. The location where the horse was buried was once Native grounds, specifically, some say, a preserved burial mound. Is this where the horse found its undead rider? The bones of both the horse and Natives were paved over in the 1960s, around the same time of the first ghost horse sightings. Understandably, this has led some to speculate that disturbing the mound was what unleashed this spectral steed.

OLD BOB

Bob was buried at his former place of employment, which gives him the distinction of being the only nonhuman ever given a plot and a tombstone at Sanford's Lakeview Cemetery. The cemetery dates to 1884, when T.J. Miller became the city's first undertaker. Bob was the Miller family's horse and was put to work for twenty-eight years, transporting bodies to their final destination. When the horse passed, Miller published an obituary for him and buried him there in the cemetery. All these years later, someone must have forgotten to let Bob know that his services are no longer needed. A staff member at the Sanford History Museum

Part of Bob's original gravestone is displayed inside the Sanford Museum after being damaged by an automobile. *Photograph by the author.*

recalled her time working for the city, when once every year or two, she would receive a panicked call from a driver who had been forced to pull off to the side of the road because a large horse had materialized from out of nowhere along the road by the cemetery. After these incidents, the horse always somehow vanished, leaving the driver confused and shaken by the encounter. There's no word on more recent sightings of Bob, but anyone driving near the old cemetery should be prepared to share the road with this phantasmal workhorse.

DEAD MAN'S OAK AND THE HEADLESS HORSEMAN (KISSIMMEE)

Legends of headless riders on horseback go back further than most folks probably realize—all the way back to Irish folklore in the form of what's called the Dullahan or Gan Cean (both described earlier on page 54). Of course, most people are more familiar with the version of this tale that was popularized in Washington Irving's classic "The Legend of Sleepy Hollow," as well as the animated film of the same name and the more-recent Tim Burton version of the tale (which features Christopher Walken as the wickedly pointy-toothed Hessian).

It turns out, there's also a similar legend involving Kissimmee, located just south of Orlando. This particular tale is thought to date back more than a century and has been passed down from generation to generation. Consequently, as with any orally transmitted tale, different versions and variations have emerged.

In the first version, Spanish soldiers in the area captured a man on a white horse near the ancient tree known as Dead Man's Oak. The man was fleeing after having committed a crime of some sort. He was caught before he could escape, and then he was tied to the tree and beheaded. Since that time, around midnight on certain nights, the white horse and rider (sans head), return and roam the area, sometimes chasing off those unlucky enough to encounter them.

As the Weird U.S. website points out, there are some obvious problems with this version of the tale, not least of which being that the place where Dead Man's Oak stands (and there isn't complete agreement on the tree's exact location) would have been controlled by Native people at the time, and no European, not even a criminal on a fast horse, would have been inclined to try to escape through that particular area.

A second version of the tale has developed, in which the horseman was not hanged for crimes against the Spanish but rather for being a cattle thief. In this variant, since the man was hanged, his ghost's head remains attached.

Ultimately, which version (if either) one chooses to believe may be a moot point. Despite internet claims that hundreds have witnessed this horseman (though it's not clear how many of those have seen him with versus without his head), as blogger Evelyn Martinez noted in her write-up on the original NewsBreak website, there have not been any fresh sightings of this particular specter since 2000.

FLICKER AND DIE: THE OVIEDO GHOST LIGHTS (OVIEDO)

Just about twenty-five minutes east of Orlando is the small town of Oviedo, which dates back to 1865, just after the Civil War, when homesteaders first arrived to settle along Lake Jesup. (Prior to this, formerly enslaved people and Swedish immigrants made the area their home. And long before them, the Natives known as the Timucua lived in the area.) On March 13, 1879, Andrew Aulin chose Oviedo (named after a city in northern Spain) as the location of the post office, and the town has been known as such ever since. In 1925, Oviedo was officially incorporated as a city with a population of eight hundred residents.

As a farming community, Oviedo produced both citrus and celery (though it was nearby Sanford that claimed for itself the title Celery City and "celery capital of the world"). Today, although neither of these two crops are grown there much beyond private backyard gardens, the legacy of those early farms lives on in another way, specifically in the large feral chicken population, which owes its size to more than one of the birds flying the coop and crossing the road. Today, as symbols of the city, the Oviedo chickens are protected by law and even have their own social media accounts.

For more than seventy years, there has also been talk of something other than wild chickens and celery stalking this small town. Those familiar with the unexplained phenomena in Central Florida have likely heard of the phenomenon known as the Oviedo ghost lights (also sometimes called the Chuluota lights).

This particular legend dates back to the 1950s, and even today, it's not uncommon to find cars parked near the bridge over the Econlockhatchee

(Econ) River between Snow Hill and Chuluota. What they're looking for are the strange lights that are said to rise up from the water, hang suspended in midair and sometimes give chase to observers.

Most agree that the lights most frequently appear between midnight and one o'clock in the morning during the warmer months of the year. Multiple credible eyewitnesses, including Christine Kinlaw-Best, have seen anywhere between one and a half-dozen balls of greenish light rise up from the water and take off down the nearby road like the headlights of an invisible car, only to stop suddenly and hang suspended in the air. The late Charlie Carlson, who documented a variety of local legends in *Weird Florida*, claimed he witnessed this for himself and described it as "a very faint, glowing ball of fog rising up from the swamp."

Author Amanda Branham connects the lights to the local legend of a man who took his own life by jumping from the bridge there after losing the woman he loved. This, she reasoned, might also be why the lights seem prone to chase lovers who wander into the area, seeking a secluded place to be together.

Many, however, feel that there are logical rather than supernatural reasons for the lights. For instance, some believe that the reason the lights are so often likened to headlights is because that's exactly what they are, an optical illusion caused by distant headlights. Others attribute the phenomenon to flammable swamp gas released from decomposing organic matter. It should be noted that just because swamp gas sounds like the sort of convenient cover-up explanation offered by some shadowy government agency in an episode of the *X-Files*, that doesn't mean it isn't actually real.

A staff member at the Sanford History Museum agrees that the lights are likely part of a natural phenomenon and points out that the Econ River and other waterways in the area have a particularly high concentration of phosphate. While she doesn't believe that the lights are proof of a haunting, she does see continuing interest in them as proof of a different tradition that is every bit as old as the telling of ghost stories. That timeless tradition? Rural kids and teenagers devising ways to have a laugh at the expense of their big-city peers.

In support of the theory that folks in Oviedo like to tell some rather tall tales is another local legend that stretches credulity to the very limit, if not well past it. This is the story of a killer named Christopher Klink (also known as "Killer Klink"), and it centers on a bridge over the Econ River. He is said to have tagged the bridge with graffiti on October 13, 1987. Shortly thereafter, believing that he had successfully beaten charges related to the murder of multiple women in the area, he was caught by the families of his victims who decided to take matters into their own hands. They delivered their own brand of justice by hanging Klink from the very bridge where he had left his name. Now, according to the legend, every October 13, temperatures near the bridge plummet, the water begins to flow backward and Klink himself appears swinging from a noose under the bridge.

Now, aside from the fact that extensive searches through print and digital archives have yielded little to support the story, it also seems that while the tale has been often repeated, it has not, to anyone's knowledge, actually been verified by any reliable, eyewitness accounts. Lastly, let's be honest, it doesn't exactly bolster the story's believability when one realizes that Killer Klink also happens to be the title of a 1967 *Hogan's Heroes* episode.

BLOOD ON THE ASPHALT: THE I-4 DEAD ZONE

Anyone who's spent enough time in Orlando will probably have heard the phrase "Old Florida." For the long-time, multigenerational area residents, that refers to a time when citrus and cattle ranching were still Orlando's major industries, long before Walt arrived to build his entertainment empire in the Sunshine State. So, what separates Old Florida from the present-day version? There's no perfect consensus, but many cite the arrival of the major highways that brought tourists into the area and forever changed the landscape. You can curse Interstate 4 (I-4) for the seemingly endless congestion it creates and for the proliferation of tacky tourist giftshops, big-box stores and global chain restaurants, but the short span located between Orlando and Daytona, according to some, has already been cursed by the spirits of the dead.

The construction of I-4 began in 1958 and was completed in 1965, since which time it has connected Tampa to Daytona Beach, running generally along a southeast–northwest path, and it has ranked consistently as one of the most dangerous highways in the state of Florida (and beyond, in 2017, it was actually named the most dangerous American highway by GPS data company Teletrac Navman)

Statistics back up that claim. An average of now more than 1.25 deaths have occurred for each of the road's 132 miles. Some portions of the highway are, of course, more prone to accidents than others, and the quarter-mile stretch in Seminole County, just before the south end of the St. Johns River Bridge (about halfway between Orlando and Daytona), has earned the name the I-4 Dead Zone. Could the high number of accidents be connected to ghost activity, and if so, what is the underlying cause?

As is to be expected, there are many variations of the story about how the I-4 Dead Zone came to be haunted. Most of these adhere, more or less, to the version outlined by author Charlie Carlson.

In 1886, the land over which I-4 now runs was owned by Henry Sanford. He had divided the land into ten-acre parcels, on which he planned to create a Roman Catholic community called St. Joseph's Colony. Felix Swembergh was selected to serve as the priest for future residents, and in the same way that he found workers to populate his own eponymous city, Sanford recruited immigrants from Europe (this time, choosing Germans rather than Swedes to live there). He met, however, with considerably less success than he expected and persuaded only four families to relocate to his nascent colony. One of these families was hit especially hard by an outbreak of yellow fever the following year.

Fearing contagion, the surviving colonists buried their dead in the woods nearby without performing last rites and without a priest in attendance (Swembergh was tending to fever victims in Tampa at the time). These burials, it seems, provide a possible origin for the area's haunted history.

By 1905, Albert S. Hawkins and his family owned the land on which the graves stood, which had become part of the town of Lake Monroe. Hawkins warned other farmers to whom he leased the land to leave the burial plot alone. Carson relates two tales of farmers who attempted, in one instance, to remove the wire fence around a grave and, in the other instance, remove the illegible, weatherworn markers themselves. In both cases, the farmers each lost their homes to fires shortly thereafter (the second farmer being Hawkins himself).

In 1959, the State of Florida became the new owner of the land (which included what had become known locally as "the field of the dead"). In September the following year, the state began dumping fill dirt over the area to elevate it for the construction of what would become Interstate 4. Allegedly, the same day the graves were covered, Hurricane Donna, which was heading through south Florida, toward the Gulf, took an unexpected turn to follow the planned route of I-4, its eye passing directly over the long-since-nameless dead, late at night on September 10, 1960. This was to be the first but not the last major storm to hit the I-4 Dead Zone. These included three in 2004 (Charley, Frances and Jeanne), as well as Hurricane Matthew in 2016, Hurricane Irma in 2017, Hurricane Dorian in 2019 and, most recently, Hurricane Ian in 2022.

The I-4 Dead Zone's tempestuous legacy extends well beyond weather-related incidents. Electrical interference has been frequently reported and includes the loss of cellular and radio signals (with ghostly voices sometimes heard through the static). Visual anomalies have been experienced as well, ranging from mists to wispy orbs of light and at least one account of "pioneer ghosts standing by the road at night."

GUIDED BY VOICES: CASSADAGA

Virtually all of the locations covered in this book share a common feature: their respective ghosts came to reside there over time as the result of unplanned and usually unfortunate circumstances. The one exception to that pattern? The village of Cassadaga, which alone can claim to have had a spirit involved in its founding.

The story begins with George P. Colby, who was born on January 6, 1848, in Pike, Alleghany County, New York. When he was a boy, his family moved first to Indiana and then to Cherry Grove, Minnesota, where George first exhibited his gift for mediumship at the age of twelve following his baptism in freezing winter lake water. This first message from the spirit realm was delivered by his deceased uncle, who informed Colby that he would one day found a great spiritual center in the South.

To the dismay of his parents, Colby, in the years following this initial experience, continued to demonstrate other unusual gifts, including clairvoyance and healing by the laying on of hands. In 1967, he broke away from the church and became a practicing medium for the next several years, offering private readings and parlor seances.

Colby moved for a time to Iowa, where the Native spirit Seneca (one of several spirit guides that communicated to Colby) instructed him to seek out a T.D. Giddings in Eau Claire, Wisconsin. Following this advice, Colby, once in Wisconsin, connected with fellow Spiritualist Theodore D. Giddings. During a séance, he was ordered to accompany Giddings to Florida to acquire land that had been selected by a "congress of spirits" for the purpose of establishing a great spiritual center. Thus, he continued the prophecy he had received from his uncle as a child.

The group traveled next to Jacksonville, and from there, they traveled by boat to Blue Springs Landing, taking lodging in the unoccupied Barontine house. Two days later, Colby was led by Seneca down a footpath to the spot

The entrance to Camp Cassadaga, circa 1900. *Courtesy of Florida Memory, State Library and Archives of Florida.*

that would become the Southern Cassadaga Spiritualist Camp Meeting Association (the charter for which was officially granted on March 28, 1884, nine years after Colby's first visit). Colby spent the final years of his life there and passed away at a nearby hospital from a stroke on July 27, 1993.

Since then, the community has grown from a small camp for visiting spiritualists to a town with full-time residents, along with a bookstore, temple and hotel. Of course, given that all of those who live there share a belief in communicating with the spirits, the absence of ghosts would probably be more unusual than their presence. Predictably, the community is said to be populated by a great many spirits, but some locations are more populous with ghosts (and more popular with those who seek them) than others.

The Cassadaga Hotel, which was originally owned by Emma J. Huff, was built in 1894 and rebuilt following a fire on Christmas 1926. According to author Dusty Smith, among those who lived, died and still reside at the hotel are the ghosts of Alice Myers and her brother Arthur, who were employed at the hotel as a maid and maintenance man. They lived there on the second floor, and after dinner, Arthur was said to enjoy a nip of gin he kept in his room. He would then head back downstairs to play the piano for his sister and the hotel's guests.

Alice, who lived in room 19, was the first of the two siblings to pass on. More than one guest, while unpacking and settling into room 19, has said that they clearly heard the voice of a woman tell them, "My name is Alice, and I belong here." More recently, some mediums think Alice has moved on, but others claim that she continues to inform guests and staff of her presence.

Experts say that Arthur is still at the hotel as well and that his footsteps can be heard descending the stairs at night. One former dishwasher claims Arthur not only met her coming down the stairs, but he also regularly brought her a shot of gin. Others have said that he turns lights on and off and that the scents of cigars and gin still waft from his former room.

"Gentleman Jack," as he's known, is the spirit of, some suspect, a traveling salesman who liked to stay in room 10 on the first floor whenever he was passing through the area. Even in death, this particular spirit has a fondness for women, to whom he makes himself known with a blast of cold air, the scent of bay rum aftershave, a tug on the clothing or hair and, every once in a while, a touch on their arms and shoulders.

Also present at the hotel are the spirits of two young sisters, Kaitlin and Sarah. (The house rule that children and minors must be accompanied by an adult does not, apparently, extend to ghosts.) They have been seen dancing in the second-floor hallways and heard giggling and singing.

Though the hotel is not pet-friendly, that has not prevented the spirit of a stray tomcat from taking up residence in room 3. Guests, while sleeping in the bed there, have been awakened by the feeling of something pouncing on the sheets, and many have either felt or briefly glimpsed a cat wandering throughout the building and sunning itself on various seats and ledges.

While researching her book about Florida's haunted locations, author Joyce Elston Moore had an unusual experience of her own, though not one directly connected to any specific ghost. While trying to photograph the exterior of the hotel, the needle on the light meter of her camera began moving wildly. When she took the camera to a local shop, no problem was found, and everything, including the light meter, seemed to be functioning properly. Afterward, Moore used the camera without any further incidents. Whatever had caused it to misbehave seemed isolated to the hotel.

On a side note, while seeking the supernatural in Cassadaga, it's worth making a stop in Deland, less than ten miles south of the Spiritualist camp. A recent addition to the local landscape and a great place to explore the area's haunted history is the Haunted Antique Shop, run by author Corrine Kenner. The shop itself is alleged to host as many as a half-dozen different ghosts, some of which are attached to the location and some of which are connected to specific objects there (the most active of which are kept in the store's Cabinet of Curiosities). Still other ghosts wander in from time to time, tethered to living visitors. Described as "gently haunted," the shop is a fun and friendly place to part the veil between worlds, and who knows, maybe you'll leave with a little something—or someone—extra.

SPACE GHOSTS: LAUNCH COMPLEX 34 (CAPE CANAVERAL)

Surely, curiosity is one of humanity's most essential and defining qualities, and for as long as we have sought some clue about what awaits us on the other side of this life, so, too, have we wondered about what lies beyond the stars. As it turns out, there is one location less than an hour east of Orlando that speaks to both of those mysteries: launch complex 34 at Cape Canaveral.

Rewind to October 4, 1957. On that date, the Soviet Union successfully launched their *Sputnik I* satellite, thereby heralding the opening of the Space Race. When President Eisenhower signed Public Law 85-568, he established the National Aeronautics and Space Administration (better known as NASA). A few years later, the Soviets took another step forward by putting the first cosmonaut into orbit. Not to be outdone, in 1961, President Kennedy announced that before the end of the decade, the United States would accomplish the goal of landing a man on the moon and then bringing him back safely to Earth.

Portrait of the *Apollo I* crew. *From left to right*: Edward H. White II, Virgil I. "Gus" Grissom and Roger B. Chaffee. *Photograph by the author, courtesy of NASA.*

Even though some at the time said this couldn't be done (and even some today remain convinced that it hasn't been done), plans were laid and set into motion. The same year Kennedy made his moonshot announcement, NASA requested appropriations to purchase two hundred square miles of land on Merritt Island in support of the Apollo Lunar Landing Program. That land became the Kennedy Space Center (or KSC).

The first U.S. Space Program, Project Mercury, ran from 1958 to 1963, with six manned flights that achieved the mission of orbiting a crewed spacecraft around the Earth and testing humans' ability to function in space. Project Apollo, NASA's next mission, was initiated in 1960 and achieved its objective, landing a total of six spacecraft carrying twelve astronauts to the lunar surface between 1969 and 1972. It did not, however, reach that goal without the tragic loss of three astronauts.

Ahead of the first manned mission in the Apollo program, which was scheduled for a February 1967 launch, a crew was selected that included experienced astronaut Ed White (an air force lieutenant colonel and first American to perform a "spacewalk"), crew commander Virgil "Gus" Grissom (an air force veteran of the Korean War and one of the Mercury Seven astronauts) and Roger Chaffee (who, despite being a navy lieutenant commander with over a decade of experience in the space program, was still considered the rookie of the three).

On January 27, 1967, the three men rode out to the launch site and boarded their spacecraft for a test of its internal power. Since the pyrotechnics had been turned off for this test, none of the engineers anticipated any danger. Still, the countdown had to be postponed when the crew detected a foul odor in the oxygen supply. While they waited inside the craft, the communications systems also started to malfunction. Then at 6:31 p.m., a fire broke out, which is believed to have been the result of a spark from faulty wiring igniting the oxygen-rich air. The pressure from the fire sealed the hatch door tight, and though a groundcrew was able to pry it open with difficulty, it was already too late for the three astronauts.

NASA spent the next eighteen months applying the lessons it learned from the tragedy to reduce flammable materials on board and to make other lifesaving design changes. Then, on October 11, 1968, the first and last manned launch from LC-34 of *Apollo VII* took place. The launch complex was decommissioned in 1971 and now serves as a memorial to the three members of the Apollo 1.

Over the years, however, some claim that those three men have not gone quietly into the hereafter. In addition to a powerful sense of unease, there

The *Apollo I* memorial at Launch Complex 34. *Photograph by Doug Ellison, courtesy of NASA.*

have been reports of a ghostly astronaut at the former launch site and screams heard emanating from the structure. It's alleged that NASA, at one point, ceased allowing visitors near the memorial due to all of the unusual activity there.

At present, taking one of the tram tours offered by the Kennedy Space Center is as close as one can get to launch complex 34. Common sense should be enough to deter most individuals from trying to sneak any closer to a secure NASA facility, complete with gates and guards. Still, should anyone need a reminder, please do not, under any circumstances, try to reach this or any other off-limit area unless you plan to add your own cries of pain and anguish to any of those already emanating from the former launch site.

BIBLIOGRAPHY

BOOKS

Branham, Amanda. *Orlando Ghosts.* Atglen, PA: Schiffer, 2009.

Brown, John, and Joshua Ginsberg. *Secret Orlando: A Guide to the Weird, Wonderful and Obscure.* St. Louis, MO: Reedy Press, 2023.

Carlson, Charlie. *Weird Florida.* Ontario, CA: Sterling Publishing, 2005.

Clark, James C. *Orlando, Florida: A Brief History.* Charleston, SC: The History Press, 2013.

Cook, Smith. *Orlando's Historic Haunts.* Sarasota, FL: Pineapple Press, 2013.

Dickey, Colin. *Ghostland: An American History in Haunted Places.* New York: Penguin Books, 2016

Jenkins, Greg. *Florida's Ghostly Legends and Haunted Folklore.* Vol. 1. Sarasota, FL: Pineapple Press, 2005.

Kenner, Corrine. *Gently Haunted: True Stories from the Haunted Antique Shop.* Woodbury, MN: Llewellyn Publications, 2022.

Lapham, Dave. *Ghosthunting Florida.* Covington, KY: Clerisy Press, 2010.

Michaels, Kara. *Haunted America: Florida.* N.p.: Witchside Books, 2023.

Moore, Joyce Elson. *Haunt Hunter's Guide to Florida.* Sarasota, FL. Pineapple Press, 1998.

Muncy, Mark, and Kari Schultz. *Creepy Florida.* Charleston, SC: The History Press, 2019.

———. *Eerie Florida.* Charleston, SC: The History Press, 2017.

———. *Freaky Florida.* Charleston, SC: The History Press, 2018.

Owens, Elizabeth. *Cassadaga Florida, Yesterday and Today*. 5th ed. Revised, Orange City, FL: Pisces Publishing, 2015.

Rappa, Ting, and Debra Walloch Hoffman. *In the Shadow of Two Theme Park Castles: Haunted Orlando*. Self-published, 2020.

Smith, Dusty. *Haunted DeLand and the Ghosts of West Volusia County*. Charleston, SC: The History Press, 2008.

Whitehead, David W. *Field Guide to Haunted Orlando*. Orlando, FL: CreateSpace, 2008.

PRINT AND DIGITAL ARTICLES

Answer Man. "Questioned Mark." *Orlando*, April 2013. https://www.orlandomagazine.com/questioned-mark/.

Branham, Amanda M. "Homegrown Haunts: Orlando Ghost Stories." *Reflections*, Fall 2015. Reprinted on the Orange County Regional History Center's *Around the Museum* blog, October 19, 2020. https://www.thehistorycenter.org/homegrown-haunts/.

D'Ambrosio, Kelly. "The Way We Were: Terror on Church Street." *Community Paper*, June 30, 2023. https://www.yourcommunitypaper.com/articles/the-way-we-were-terror-on-church-street/.

FOX 35 News. "10 Scary Urban Legends, Haunted Places to Visit in Central Florida." October 11, 2022. https://www.fox35orlando.com/news/10-central-florida-urban-legends-haunted-places-just-in-time-for-spooky-season.

Hinton, William Dean. "Last Days of Bohemia." *Orlando Weekly*, August 2, 2001. https://www.orlandoweekly.com/news/last-days-of-bohemia-2261895.

Knight, Laura. "The Barber-Mizell Feud." Once a Knight Is Enough. https://laura-knight-jadczyk.com/genealogy/barber-mizell-feud.html.

Kubersky, Seth. "Old Town Haunted History Walking Tour." *Orlando Weekly*, February 25, 2014.

Orlando Weekly. "Orlando Horror Stories: 36 of the Most Haunted Places in Central Florida." October 8, 2015. https://www.orlandoweekly.com/orlando/orlando-horror-stories-36-of-the-most-haunted-places-in-central-florida/Slideshow/30946121/30844092.

Peters, Lucia. "These 9 Disney Park Ghost Stories Will Make You Lose Sleep Tonight." *Bustle*, October 20, 2017. https://www.bustle.com/p/9-

ghosts-that-reportedly-haunt-disney-parks-from-urban-legends-to-actual-events-in-the-parks-history-2938656.

Phantom History. "Orange County Regional History Center." YouTube, May 15, 2023. https://www.youtube.com/watch?v=amz0GGUjT1c.

Roadtrippers. "An Abandoned, Believed Haunted, NASA Launch Site You Can Actually Visit." *Huffpost*, December 6, 2017. https://www.huffpost.com/entry/abandoned-places_b_4097586.

Rosen Inn. "Haunted of Hoax: Seven Spooky Places in Orlando." https://www.roseninn7600.com/blog/haunted-or-hoax-seven-spooky-places-in-orlando.

Spook Eats. "Florida: Ghosts of Walt Disney World." July 25, 2018. https://spookeats.com/2018/06/25/florida-ghosts-of-walt-disney-world/.

Weidman, Rich. "10 Most Haunted Places in Florida to Spook Your Summer Vacation!" Westgate Resorts. September 24, 2022. www.westgateresorts.com/blog/10-haunted-places-florida/.

World of Micah. "The Most HAUNTED Spots In ORLANDO, FL." YouTube, October 29, 2021. https://www.youtube.com/watch?v=6h0t29lkah0.

Zizo, Christie. "Find a Ghostly Encounter at These 15 Haunted Places in Central Florida." Click Orlando.com. October 24, 2023. https://www.clickorlando.com/news/local/2022/10/10/find-a-ghostly-encounter-at-these-15-haunted-places-in-central-florida/.

OTHER WEBSITES AND RESOURCES

City of Winter Park. https://cityofwinterpark.org/.

Haunted Places. https://www.hauntedplaces.org.

Haunted Rooms America. https://www.hauntedrooms.com/florida/orlando/haunted-places.

Orlando Memory. https://orlandomemory.info/.

Winter Park Chamber of Commerce. https://winterpark.org/.

About the Author

Joshua Ginsberg is an author and curiosity seeker. He has written multiple local travel and history books, including *Haunted Orlando* (2024) and *Secret Tampa Bay: A Guide to the Weird, Wonderful and Obscure* (2020), and he coauthored *Secret Orlando: A Guide to the Weird, Wonderful and Obscure* (2023). His work has also appeared in print and digital publications such as *Trembling with Fear* (*The Horror Tree*), the *Chamber Magazine*, the *City Key*, 365tomorrows, *Atlas Obscura*, *Travel After Five*, and on his own blog, *Terra Incognita Americanus*. He lives in Tampa with his wife, Jen, and their Shih Tzu, Tinker Bell.

FREE eBOOK OFFER

Scan the QR code below, enter your e-mail address and get our original Haunted America compilation eBook delivered straight to your inbox for free.

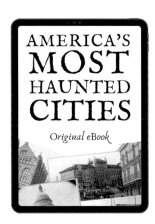

ABOUT THE BOOK

Every city, town, parish, community and school has their own paranormal history. Whether they are spirits caught in the Bardo, ancestors checking on their descendants, restless souls sending a message or simply spectral troublemakers, ghosts have been part of the human tradition from the beginning of time.

In this book, we feature a collection of stories from five of America's most haunted cities: Baltimore, Chicago, Galveston, New Orleans and Washington, D.C.

SCAN TO GET
AMERICA'S MOST HAUNTED CITIES

Having trouble scanning? Go to:
biz.arcadiapublishing.com/americas-most-haunted-cities